THE LAWN GUIDE

— THE EASY WAY TO A PERFECT LAWN —

Sharples & Hayman

For Kit, Brooke, James, Jade, Ingrid, Chris, David, Thomas & Katie Louise

Website: www.thelawnguide.com
Email: info@thelawnguide.com
Tel: 07854 981744

Acknowledgements

Special thanks go to:

Laurence Gale MSc and www.pitchcare.com for their donation of pictures

Lee Jackson – Pictures of fantastic mowing patterns at Manchester City FC

Chris Mitchell – Picture of leatherjackets

Pam Sherratt, Dr. D. Gardner and **Prof. T. K. Danneberger** of Ohio State University, Turf grass Extension for the many disease symptom pictures

Randell G. Prostak – University of Massachusetts

CH Grounds Maintenance Ltd. for the picture of a 'verti-drain'. www.chgrounds.com

THE LAWN GUIDE

— THE EASY WAY TO A PERFECT LAWN —

CONTENTS

FOREWORD

. . . .

The term 'Lawn care' will mean different things to different people
and the amount of care a lawn receives will depend on several factors
such as time available, the purpose for which the lawn was created, the
use to which it is put and the interest of the person maintaining it.

The Lawn Guide has been written to address all of these situations
with the specific purpose of aiding and guiding the amateur,
the professional gardener and the connoisseur through the
complexities of creating their first lawn and on to maintaining
it with the care and attention it deserves and needs.

This guide gives the very best advice to all kinds of people with
all kinds of needs – from a father with three boys, no time and a
football match taking place on it, every evening after school – to the
retired couple who want to mow it every day, who take offence at
the slightest hint of moss or pest invasion and take pride in looking
at their lawn's perfect stripes, every day throughout the Summer.

So, whether you want an ornamental lawn or a functional,
family focused utility area – whatever your need, question or
requirement – the answer, together with explanation, advice
and practical tips, is all here in The Lawn Guide.

THE LAWN GUIDE – YOUR PATHWAY TO THE PERFECT LAWN

PLANNING YOUR LAWN

A lawn is established to form a long-lasting and attractive green space and will be an area that compliments and sets off any border planting and allows easy access to the majority of the garden. It can provide an extension to the living space of your home, somewhere you can relax in the summer and a focal point that you and others can admire all year around.

People grow and maintain lawns for many different reasons. Lawns not only beautify their surroundings but also help prevent soil erosion and during spells of hot weather, they cool the surrounding air making the garden a more comfortable place to be. Lawns absorb sound and produce fresh oxygen for us to breathe while also providing us with an outdoor playing facility or an extension to our living space. A successful lawn will be one that grows evenly and uniformly while exhibiting an even colour and texture throughout the year.

A well maintained and tended lawn will prove to be a valuable asset. Not only can the quality of your lawn

Fig. 1 – A poorly managed lawn

Fig. 2 – A well managed lawn

add value to your home but it will allow the gardener to enhance the appearance of their entire garden.

Types of lawn

Turfgrass Lawns (or the grasses within them) can be chosen and selected to give us the lawn that best suits our needs. Lawns can be broken down into three different types -

1. Ornamental – this type of lawn is grown for appearance only and should always look at its best. It will require the greatest amount of maintenance and manicuring, will incorporate the finest textured grasses and be dense and uniform in growth and colour. Ornamental lawns are cut very close and require the highest levels of commitment.

2. Leisure - these lawn types are designed to give the best of both worlds. Like the ornamental lawn their appearance should be fine textured and dense, but they should also allow a fair level of practicality so must be able to withstand wear and tear from foot traffic.

3. Utility – these lawn types should be very hard wearing and allow for many hours of games or play to be carried out on them while keeping a good general appearance throughout. These lawns are suitable for children and pets alike.

Size and shape

The size and shape of a lawn will largely be determined by the amount of land available for use. Even with the smallest amount of land there is scope for the gardener to create an interesting and individual design as an alternative to the more traditional rectangular or square shape. When deciding upon the shape of the lawn, consideration should be given to the gardens existing features such as the existing or proposed border planting, trees and fencing. The new shape chosen should be one that will allow (a) ease of mowing (b) as much freedom from shade as possible (c) avoidance from wet, very poorly drained areas and (d) allow access on and off the lawn. It is worth noting that narrow access routes onto busy lawned areas will generally kill off the grass or become mud baths over winter due to the wear that is received.

It is a well known and an unfortunate fact that many amateur gardeners do not pay sufficient time and attention to the initial planning, preparation and maintenance needs of the lawn and, inevitably, many lawns either fail or do not perform as required.

Choosing the right grasses

The correct choice of grass plant for its growing environment is essential for successful growth, development and the areas aesthetic value in future years. It is intended that this initial section will aid you with species and cultivar selection and help you understand the many environmental aspects that will influence growth. Perhaps the most important of these being the choice of grass species for the chosen application or characteristics required from the lawn. Many people think about aspects of soil type preferred, light conditions required plus more for other garden plants they purchase, why not for your grasses? If you are going to manage something it is best to know what you are managing, wouldn't you agree?

There are many uses for turf grasses, from lawns to sports turf applications such as football to rugby, polo or tennis, they are used in landscaping,

FIG. 3 – A TYPICAL SMALL FRONT LAWN. LAWNS BEAUTIFY THE GARDEN.

FIG. 4 – UN-MOWN GRASS

Growing habits of grasses

Grasses can grow in three different ways: (a) tufted – produce new growth from the base of the plant (b) stoloniferous – produce new growth via runners along the soils surface and, although these will be connected to the mother plant, each can develop into a new plant in its own right and (c) Rhizomatous – produce new growth via runners that grow outward under the soils surface. The stoloniferous and rhizomatous grasses tend to cope with high wear situations best.

The following pages outline some of the growing characteristics that today's most popular species and cultivars exhibit. Each table is specific to different uses for the lawn types – *ornamental*, *leisure* and *utility*. The tables will help you with

for road verges, airfields and building surrounds even orchards. Each grass species will have its benefits and disadvantages so choosing the correct species for your situation will be vital for success.

Let's now consider the best types of grass species for different lawn/turf grass area situations.

Why is one type of grass different from another?

At first glance most lawn grasses look alike. However, there are differences in growth habit that make some grasses more suited to specific purposes. There are around 360 grass genus (mother plants) and more than 10,000 species (variations, but related to the mother plants) in the world. Dwarf, fine-leafed varieties are better suited to ornamental lawns and strong growing, tough grasses with broader leaves, are better for situations where play is likely to take place. Some grasses are tuft forming and less suited to fine lawns, while others spread by creeping stolons' or rhizomes'. Finally, annual types are less suitable than perennial types… for lawns.

choosing the grass species that best suits your needs and situation.

When choosing grasses at a garden centre or supplier there will be a number of grasses ready mixed and packaged for consumer purchase.

Take a careful look at the grass species included in the mix and use table 1, 2 or 3 to ensure the product is right for your needs. You may also use the tables to help you select the correct grade of turf if you are purchasing from a turf supplier. The supplier (if they are credible) will be able to tell you exactly which grass species come with their different blends and turf types.

Grass Species	Botanical name	Growing habit	Nutrient requirement	Colour	Maintenance requirement	Leaf texture	Minimum cutting height
Strong creeping red fescue	Festuca rubra ssp. rubra	Rhizomes	Low	Medium to dark green	Medium	Fine	10mm
Slender creeping red fescue	Festuca rubra ssp. litoralis	Rhizomes	Low	Medium to dark green	Medium to low	Fine	5mm
Chewing's fescue	Festuca rubra ssp. commutata	Dense tufted	Low	Green	Medium	Fine	5mm
Brown top bent	Agrostis tenuis or capillaries	Slender stolons and rhizomes	Medium	Medium green	Medium / high	Medium / fine	5mm
Highland bent	Agrostis castellana	Rhizomes	Medium / low	Green	Medium	Medium / fine	5mm
Creeping bent	Agrostis stolonifera	Stolons	High	Green	High	Medium / fine	<5mm
Velvet bent	Agrostis canina	Stolons	Medium	Dark green	High	Medium / fine	5mm

TABLE 1 – SUGGESTED GRASSES FOR ORNAMENTAL LAWNS

Grass Species	Botanical name	Growing habit	Nutrient requirement	Colour	Maintenance requirement	Leaf texture	Minimum cutting height
Perennial rye grass	Lolium perenne	Tufted	Medium	Dark green	Medium	Medium	5 – 25mm dependant on cultivar
Smooth meadow grass	Poa pratensis	Rhizomes	Medium	Dark green	Medium	Medium	10mm
Small leaved timothy	Phleum bertolonii	Tufted sometimes stolons	Medium	Green	Medium	Medium	20mm
Creeping bent	Agrostis stolonifera	Stolons	High	Green	High	Medium / fine	< 5mm
Velvet bent	Agrostis canina	Stolons	Medium	Dark green	High	Medium / fine	5mm
Brown top bent	Agrostis tenuis or capillaries	Slender stolons and rhizomes	Medium	Medium green	Medium / high	Medium / fine	5mm

TABLE 2 – SUGGESTED GRASSES FOR LEISURE LAWNS (APPEARANCE AND PRACTICALITY)

Grass Species	Botanical name	Growing habit	Nutrient requirement	Colour	Maintenance requirement	Leaf texture	Minimum cutting height
Slender creeping red fescue	Festuca rubra ssp. litoralis	Rhizomes	Low	Medium to dark green	Medium to low	Fine	5mm
Sheep's fescue	Festuca ovina	Dense tufted	Low	Blue/green	Medium to low	Fine	25mm
Chewing's fescue	Festuca rubra ssp. commutate	Dense tufted	Low	Green	Medium	Fine	5mm
Brown top bent	Agrostis tenuis or capillaries	Slender stolons and rhizomes	Medium	Medium green	Medium / high	Medium / fine	5mm
Creeping bent	Agrostis stolonifera	Stolons	High	Green	High	Medium / fine	< 5mm
Perennial rye grass	Lolium perenne	Tufted	Medium	Dark green	Medium	Medium	5 – 25mm dependant on cultivar

TABLE 3 - SUGGESTED GRASSES FOR UTILITY LAWNS (HIGH USE, HEAVY WEAR)

PREPARING THE SITE

Site preparation is just as important (if not more so) to the final outcome and future health of your lawn as the choice of the correct grass species. The aim should be to create a level, firm and free draining surface on which to sow your seed or plant your turf.

The soil type the lawn grows upon will determine how well the grass thrives in its new environment. Soils determine how water, nutrients and air are held within them and the grass plant requires each of these in order to grow to its fullest potential. Excess or lack of these will eventually lead to the demise of the plant.

Whether sowing seed or laying turf, careful preparation of the lawn site is essential. If sowing seed, a fine, crumb-like soil structure (known as a fine tilth) must be achieved on the surface because without this the seedlings or the roots from the turf will struggle to grow after germination. The lawn site must also be leveled otherwise the final matured turf levels will be uneven. Lawns may be sown or laid at

SPRING	The time to sow seed or lay turf, prepare seed beds and cultivate the soil to a good fine tilth – A fine tilth can be established through thoroughly raking the soil breaking all the clods of soil into pea size crumbs
SUMMER	The ideal time to fallow the soil – leave bare and kill weeds as they appear to prevent infestation later. Complete any planning work at this time and perhaps cultivate the soil
AUTUMN	Prepare the soil, sow seed or lay turf
WINTER	Best for planning only, however turf may be laid at this time with care

TABLE 4 – WORK BY SEASON

anytime of the year although the two favoured seasons for sowing grass seed are spring and autumn. This timing is suggested as the soil is relatively warm and contains adequate amounts of moisture to ensure quick germination and establishment. If proper irrigation is applied then summer planting can be desirable because the germination and establishment of the sward will be quick and effective.

Turf can be laid at almost anytime of the year and even during colder periods the turf will still develop a root system even when the leaf is dormant. As with laying turf,

summer sowing of seed can be carried out so long as irrigation is applied.

Preparatory work by season

Creating a high quality lawn involves careful attention to soil preparation so that it will allow healthy turf growth. The operations that are normally required are:

1. Clear the site of any debris, trees, shrubs or unwanted growth

2. Grade or level the site to the desired final levels

3. Drain the site if necessary

4. Cultivate or improve the soil by adding organic matter or sand

5. Carry out final seed bed preparations such as final leveling, fertilising or producing a fine tilth to the soil. (Fig. 5)

Soil preparation should be completed as far in advance of the sowing or turfing date as possible. Ideally, at least a month should be left between preparing the soil and sowing the seed or planting the turf, to allow for any final settling of the soil following the initial 'heeling in'. Two days before the seed is sown or turf is laid the final preparations to the soil should commence. In the case of seeding, a fine soil crumb should be achieved by raking. (Fig. 5)

Clearing the site

Newer gardens are often covered with builder's rubble, while older gardens may be covered with weeds or other unwanted vegetation. Whatever the type of debris you have it must be cleared away completely before any operations can begin. Rubble or large stones must be taken 'off site' and any smaller stones must also be removed because they will only cause problems (expensive problems!) later with your mower blades or become a danger to those using the lawn.

Any unwanted vegetation should be removed or, ideally, killed using a total weed killer containing glyphosate (use when plants are growing actively). Always ensure you follow manufacturer's recommendations when using herbicides and wear the correct safety equipment. Other methods of clearing unwanted growth without the use of herbicides, are to to use a flame gun or to skim off the surface vegetation with a spade. However, in both instances only the top growth is killed and not the roots. Also, flame guns are dangerous to use and using a spade does no favours to those who suffer with bad backs!

The bare soil

Once all the surface debris has been removed you should be left with a bare soil site. At this stage it is worth noting the depth of top-soil you have throughout the garden area. (You can do this by pushing a spade into the soil and noting how deep it penetrates). Ideally, there should be a top-soil depth of between 10 - 30cm throughout. Look for where the soil changes colour from brown (typically top-soil) to a light brown or red colour (typically sub-soil). If your garden has no or little top-soil, then you need to find a supply which is the same or similar to that already in place. Take a sample to your local supplier and they will be able to advise you on the best soil to buy.

If your garden has poor drainage laying a new lawn provides an opportunity to improve it by purchasing a good quality sand and rotovating it into the top-soil. Sandy soils can drain very quickly so it may be necessary to apply more than usual amounts of water and nutrient to the site once the turf is established.

When levelling your lawn there are a number of points that need to be considered: (a) will the site slope towards your house – if so you may find flooding occurs during heavy rain; (b) the better your levelling, the better the quality of finish you will achieve when mowing (c) avoid leaving hollows and humps and bumps, these will lead to poor aesthetics once the lawn has been mowed. The hollows will act as a water trap and the humps are likely to dry out rapidly during dry spells (d) contours are acceptable on larger lawns so long as they are uniform and smooth.

Cultivating and improving soil

Cultivating soil may mean breaking it up from its existing state, adding nutrients and checking the drainage – both for excessive water holding and for drought symptoms.

With regard to a poorly draining soil, the tell-tale signs are a soil that is grey-blue in colour, may smell like rotten eggs (stagnant) or you constantly find puddles appearing around your feet when walking over the site.

If there are problems with drainage of the site then it may be necessary to install a drainage system into the soil. However, these can be very difficult and expensive to install and it is best advised to contact a drainage specialist to carry out the work. It is worth noting that a DIY drainage job may well lead to a lot of effort for very little gain because a drainage system must be designed and installed to match the existing soil type and the fall of land to work effectively. Also, the outlet for the drained water must be suitably sited and environmentally sound.

The cheapest and simplest methods to improve soil conditions for drainage will be: (a) to incorporate sand into the soil through use of a cultivator - the sand will improve the soils permeability; (b) cultivate the soil using a rotovator – this will improve the structure of the soil and allow more rapid drainage or, (c) if you do not want to go to the expense of installing any drainage system at all, just accept that the lawn may sometimes be too wet to use. Regular aeration work (see page 55) will improve and help maintain good drainage properties for the soil.

The opposite may also be the case with some soils naturally being very dry (typically those containing a lot of sand). These may have to be improved through adding organic matter into the soil using a cultivator or through the more time consuming method of single digging, then incorporating organic matter, or even some good quality top-soil. This will significantly enhance the water and nutrient holding qualities of the soil.

Whatever the drainage qualities of the soil, for the best results in later years the bare soil should be cultivated to improve its structure. This can be carried out manually using a spade or fork (through turning the soil – although this is very time consuming) or through use of a cultivator (most hire shops supply these). If you do choose a machine to do the cultivating works, try to avoid making too fine a tilth and over working the soil (good for the sowing stage but not at this stage) as a fine soil tends to cap or compact easily. Rotary blade cultivators also leave a very loose soil that will need firming before sowing seed. Firming of the soil can be achieved by walking all over the site (at least twice) on your heels (or with your weight directed down toward your heels) followed by levelling with a rake.

Final preparations

As the time to sow seed or lay turf gets nearer the focus should be on producing the perfect seed bed. Rough cultivation work (big soil clods or lumps) need breaking down further with the back of a fork and then the site raked to produce a fine tilth (pea sized soil crumbs). Now the surface is fairly fine you should once again remove any large and medium size stones that have been brought up to the surface and remove all the unwanted debris such as twigs , roots and weed. The easiest way to do this is with a rake.

The soil and site should now be level and smooth and ready for heeling in once again. At this stage, if you laid the turf or sow the seed without heeling at all, then the soil will settle itself over the coming months and the lawn end up with humps and hollows over the surface.

If the lawn is to establish and grow quickly, the grass plant needs a readily available supply of nutrients so, before sowing or turfing the lawn, it is wise to apply a good general fertiliser to the site (for fertiliser choice see page 49). The fertiliser will help the lawn quickly establish into a dense carpet. Without fertiliser the lawn may take longer to establish which in turn. May allow weeds to re-establish themselves.

Ideally, a pre-seed fertiliser should contain the nutrients nitrogen (N), phosphorus (P) and potassium (K) at a ratio of 15:20:15. Applications containing nitrogen are not necessarily as important when seeding but are vital when turfing. Most garden centres can supply a good pre-seed fertiliser. The fertiliser should be raked and watered into the ground then left for a few days before your seeding or turfing operations begin.

Planting the lawn

Sowing seed

Grass seed can be sowed either by hand or by using a seeder (fertiliser spreader). The seed should be spread using a criss-cross pattern to ensure an even and level coverage. When doing this, half the seed should be spread while walking in one direction and then the other half at 90° to this. Once the seed has been spread over the entire surface it should be very lightly raked into the top of the seed bed to ensure good contact

Nearly 100% sand rooting zone (Picture courtesy of Lee Jackson MCFC)

with the soil. You may then roll it lightly with a roller or a lawn mower (blades not engaged) and you may consider lightly dressing the surface with a compatible top-soil, This is not as essential for establishment as ensuring good soil/seed contact is!

A more accurate method for sowing seed by hand is to string out or to score into the entire area to be seeded, areas of one metre square. The seed can then be divided in accordance with the instructions and evenly spread over the pre-marked areas. This not only ensures even spread of seed, but also ensures that growth over the entire site will be even and uniform.

If you decide to apply the seed through a fertiliser spreader, it will need calibrating before use. The first step is to establish how to change

settings on the spreader you have purchased and then set it on the middle setting. The next step is to determine the sowing rate to be used (see 'suggested sowing rates' below or refer to the manufacturers guidance on the seed packet).

The second step involves either marking out an area one metre square with chalk on a smooth concrete or similar surface or placing a suitable cloth or sheet (one metre square) on a level surface. Walk the spreader over the area while applying seed and either sweep up and weigh (or carefully pick up the one metre square cloth and weigh the contents) to establish the output of the spreader. The applied rate should be half that recommended by the manufacturer because you will be applying the seed in two directions over the site. Adjust the settings

accordingly until you apply the correct weight of seed

Suggested sowing rates

Ryegrass (*Lolium perenne*) mixtures - 50 – 70g m²

Fescue/bent mixtures (*Festuca/Agrostis sp.*) - 35g m²

Bents only (*Agrostis sp.*) - 10 – 15g m²

Laying turf

The entire site should be well watered for at least one week before laying the turf and, also, before beginning to lay the turf, it is advised to lay out scaffolding planks to walk over the site, This will prevent any soil compaction occurring. To avoid any new laid turf being squashed or dented under the weight of your body, the planks should also be walked on when laying.

FIG. 5 – A GOOD SOIL CRUMB

The turf should be laid in a brick-like fashion (butted and matched right next to the previous piece) to ensure it knits together well. Begin by laying a row of turfs along the most accessible side of the soil bed using a tautly stretched garden line as a guide to keep the initial rows straight and uniform.

Always ensure that the turfs are laid as closely as possible to the previous turf and always work forwards facing the un-turfed area. The staggered (brick-like) effect is achieved by using a half-turf at the start and end of each successive row. When laying turf toward the edge of the lawn try not to place very small pieces right on the edge because very small, cut pieces of turf tend to dry out and die quickly.

Ideally, the turf should be laid so that it runs over the proposed edge of the lawn and only cut back once the entire surface has been placed. This can be done with a sharp turf cutting tool, such as an edging iron, to establish the edge or lawn boundary. You can use the scaffolding planks to achieve a straight edge or an old garden hose to establish less formal shaped, edges. Do not be afraid to cut the turf just ensure that all the edges are well matched and butted together closely once cutting is complete.

After care

Keep traffic (of any kind) off the newly sown area for about one month after sowing and for about two weeks after turfing. Ensure adequate water is applied to the newly turfed or seeded area because the first two months are vital germination/rooting periods. The grass plant consists of

POST GERMINATION PRACTICES

If the lawn was established with seed then roll to consolidate the surface after germination has taken place and prior to the initial cut. This will push any small stones into the surface and induce tillering (production of new leaves) of the plants. Can be done with a cylinder mower with the height of cut disengaged or raised. Large stones will need to be hand picked firstly.

First cut – Give the first cut once the grass blades are at a height of 25 mm (fine grasses), 50 mm (coarser grasses). Use a rotary mower and remove debris. Keeping a high height of cut for the first 6 months will benefit root development

Ensure removal of all broad-leaved weeds by hand. After three or four months it will be possible to spray using a selective herbicide.

Feed the sward the following spring with a fertiliser high in Nitrogen and Potassium but low in Phosphorus.

TABLE 5 – POST GERMINATION PRACTICES

Problem	Remedy/Action
Weeds	Hand pick out. Also read pages 67–73
Thin / sparse grass growth	Leave for at least 1 month, if still thin, rake to lightly break up exposed soil surface and re-seed
Uneven surface	Top dress uneven areas by hand and re-seed.
Disease	See page 75
Cracks	Water dry soil frequently, rake and re-seed
Turf shrinkage	Caused by insufficient watering after laying, water, if ends are dead, cut away, apply dressing to holes and seed
Wet / sodden patches	Fork the sodden areas, apply sand dressing, and work the sand into holes.
Stones	Rake up and remove as necessary
Yellow turf/weak growing	May need light fertilisation. Water in fertiliser well.

TABLE 6 – NEW LAWN PROBLEMS

over 85% water, so it is essential for growth and development.

Watering should be carried out frequently enough to ensure that the area does not dry out and the soil stays in a moist, but not flooded condition. After two months you can revert to heavier, less frequent, applications of water to the area.

Problems with new lawns

Even with the best preparation and timing new lawns can sometimes encounter problems. Table 6 identifies some of the common problems and the control measures needed to correct them.

LAWN MAINTENANCE OPERATIONS

Introduction

This chapter considers the timing of the maintenance operations needed to produce a quality lawn that displays the characteristics of being dense, visually pleasing, uniform in colour, texture and growth, while retaining the ability to tolerate wear and tear. The operations most frequent associated with lawn care are those of mowing and watering. - although in themselves, these do not directly guarantee the growth and development of a healthy, vigorous sward.

In fact, to fully guarantee the long-term quality of grass health and development required, care and attention must be paid to the minor operations, detailed in the following pages.

The most vital aspect for obtaining a high quality turf surface is the hard work put in by the owner of the lawn They must have an appreciation of the growing habits and characteristics of grass, the effect

FIG. 6 – A SISIS SCARIFIER

and consequences of user wear upon the surface, an understanding of how and why each maintenance task is carried out and an understanding of the way the grass plant will respond to each (again, as outlined in this book). Armed with this knowledge a quality turf grass surface will be well within reach.

Anyone can grow grass and create a lawn, but it takes skill and a lot of patience and interest to grow

a quality lawn. There is always something to do on a lawn and within the following pages you will find; a 'quick glance' guide to the maintenance year (Table 7), a brief, but very concise summary of each maintenance operation and our detailed, step-by-step guide to the maintenance year. From this point forward you will find all the lawn care maintenance facts and information you could ever need to know. The advice given here may not be 100% relevant to your lawn, but you should try the programme then develop your own to suit your particular situation. Each month has suggestions for work which might be carried out and you should note that as long as the grass keeps growing you should be prepared to mow the lawn. Even if it's to simply tidy its appearance during the colder winter months.

The maintenance year at a glance

MOWING (PAGES 35-40) – Mowing should be carried out according to growth. In reality there should be no set time for commencing mowing operations and similarly, finishing them. Mowing operations should be dependant upon the growth levels occurring. Removal of clippings can increase the amount of fertiliser needing to be applied to the lawn over the year. The higher the height of cut is set the stronger the plant will become. Even a 1 mm increase in height will enable the grass plant to photosynthesise more efficiently and, because the plant root depth is proportional to leaf growth, rooting improvements will also occur.

IRRIGATION (PAGES 45-48) – Irrigation practices should encourage root growth and help maintain good colour. Heavy and infrequent applications are best. Irrigation should only be carried out when necessary because over-watering can be just as detrimental as under-watering.

FEED (PAGES 49-54) – Spring and the early Autumn are the optimum periods of root and shoot growth. Correct fertiliser application at these times will vastly improve the colour, density and quality of a lawn, while ensuring fast recovery of any wear and tear that may have occurred.

Very light applications of nitrogen or iron during the summer period (so long as the lawn is irrigated) will also improve growth rates and leaf colour.

AERATION (PAGES 55-58) – Aeration is vital for root growth and general plant development. It is usually carried out in the Spring and Autumn but can also be carried out during the summer period because it is during this time that the oxygen demand from the soil is high. Aeration will result in better plant growth and the naturally occurring process of thatch reduction. Aeration work carried out during the colder months will improve water infiltration rates into the soil and speed up the rate at which it moves through the soil (percolation). This will help keep the surface relatively dry while allowing the soil to warm up quickly when spring arrives, thereby encouraging good growth.

	Mow	Irrigate	Feed	Aerate	Scarify	Top-dress	Weed control	Disease control	Moss control	Apply seed	Lay turf
January								If needed			
February	☑			☑				If needed			☑
March	✓	☑		☑			✓	If needed		☑	☑
April	✓	✓	✓	✓	☑	☑	✓	If needed	✓	✓	✓
May	✓	✓	☑	☑	✓	✓	✓	If needed		✓	✓
June	✓	✓	☑	☑		☑	☑	If needed			☑
July	✓	✓		☑		☑	☑	If needed			☑
August	✓	✓	☑	☑		✓	✓	If needed		☑	☑
September	✓	✓	✓	✓	✓	☑	✓	If needed	✓	✓	✓
October	✓	☑		☑		☑	✓	If needed		☑	☑
November	✓	☑		☑				If needed		☑	☑
December								If needed			

TABLE 7 – THE MAINTENANCE YEAR ✓ = IDEAL TIME ☑ = POSSIBLE

SCARIFICATION AND VERTI-CUTTING (PAGES 59-62) – Both of these can be carried out as frequently as required to remove and control thatch. The procedure to follow is to work in no more than two directions each time with the second pass being at 45o to the first. If scarification is to be carried out frequently (if thatch accumulation is a problem) it is advisable to operate in one direction only. The grass plant must be growing vigorously to ensure speedy recovery from damage. To assist, a light application of fertiliser two weeks prior to scarifying can be made. Verti-cutting is a lighter, less damaging operation and can be carried out more frequently. Irrigation will be vital to ensure recovery after this operation. Scarification/verti-cutting operations can also be used to remove moss after a suitable moss killer has been applied.

TOP-DRESSING (PAGES 63-66) – For the ornamental lawn, top-dressing should be carried out at least once each year. If the dressing is applied heavily after aeration practices such as hollow-tining, then it can improve the soils texture, structure, drainage and aeration properties. Frequent light dressings are also recommended if a smooth surface is required because they will help prevent thatch build-up

WEED CONTROL (PAGES 67-74) – To achieve a truly, dense and uniform lawn, surface weeds will need controlling periodically. The best defence against weed growth will be a dense turf surface that prevents the weed seeds from obtaining light, thereby preventing them germinating.

DISEASE CONTROL (PAGES 75-80) – Diseases can be a problem at any time of the year and one of the best defences is to maintain sound and regular maintenance practices month by month and season by season. So, for example ensure that applications of nitrogen are carried out at the right time of the year and in the correct dosage; that the top dressing used has the correct pH level; and, that irrigation is carried out regularly and correctly. Other influences are environmental and beyond control so, factors such as soil and air temperature, humidity, excess shade, too low or too high soil pH., can only be countered by ensuring a sound regime of maintenance practices are in place and followed.

MOSS CONTROL (PAGES 87-88) – The most effective season to treat moss is the autumn although control can also be achieved during spring. The whole moss plant should be dead before attempting to remove it from the sward.

RENOVATION – Any renovation work on the lawn is best carried out during spring and/or autumn when shoot and root growth is at its peak due to the naturally occurring high moisture levels and raised temperatures associated with these seasons. Time spent at this time of the year is worthwhile because it will prepare and repair the lawn for the coming season.

IRRIGATION IN DRY WEATHER (PAGES 45-48) From late Spring to Autumn irrigation should be applied immediately after any seeding or turfing because of the threat of dry weather. Application of seed in early spring must be complemented throughout the summer with sensible watering practices otherwise the young grasses are in danger of dying through drying out.

What to do in
JANUARY

■ TOOLS

Service and prepare mower and tools. Lightly oil all moving parts to prevent rust and clean the mower thoroughly by removing all dead/built up grass from the body and moving parts. Remember to do this with the machine un-plugged or with the spark plug HT lead removed.

■ EDGES

Establish the lawn edges with a half-moon tool (edging iron) or edging shears as necessary.

■ DEBRIS

Remove any debris that may have accumulated on the lawn.

■ DISEASE

Look out for signs of disease, especially Fusarium patch (Microdochium nivale) (see pages 75-76 for identification).

■ LEVELS

It is possible to repair and adjust turf levels during this month. Either peel back the turf (using suitable tools) and add a suitable soil* beneath or lightly dress the depression(s) with a suitable soil. If dressing the depressions, make sure you do not suffocate the turf by covering it completely. Always brush the dressing to enable the grass leaves to break through.

■ WEEDS

Pick out some weeds by hand every time you inspect the lawn. Before you know it, many of the troublesome weeds will have been removed without the use of any herbicides.

■ PETS

Dog urine can be an issue at this time of year due to the dormancy of the grass plant. Heavily water the worst affected areas. This is particularly effective if well watered just after the 'offence' has occurred! Tiresome job though!

■ FROST

Keep off the lawn when it is covered with frost. Walking on the lawn at this time will encourage 'frost burn'. Frost burn occurs when your footprints damage the plant cells of the frozen grass under the compression of your weight. After the frost has lifted you may see blackened foot impressions over the surface. However, the plant will recover from this naturally.

***Suitable soil** – a soil that is in similar quality and texture to the top-soil in which the grass plant is growing. A good place to find a soil of the correct type is in the flower or shrub beds around the perimeter of the lawn.*

What to do in

FEBRUARY

■ WORMS

Check for worm activity. Brush off any worm castings with a stiff broom. It is best to wait until the surface is dry before attempting this. Brushing sodden worm castings will only smear the exposed soil into the surface.

Unfortunately, at the time of writing this book, there are no legal effective treatments for worms available. All the effective pesticides have now been taken off the market. It is possible to discourage worm activity on the surface by spraying the fungicide 'carbendizim' because this has the effect of irritating the worms, preventing them from surfacing and therefore casting.

See the section on worms on page 82.

■ DEBRIS

Rake up and remove any dead growth with a suitable 'spring tine' rake.

■ TURF

Complete any major turfing projects before the month ends and during periods of good weather. Ensure the soil is in a suitable, relatively dry state, before attempting any major soil works.

■ DISEASE

Look out for signs of disease (see pages 75-79).

■ FROST

Keep off the lawn when it is covered with frost. Walking on the lawn at this time will encourage 'frost burn'. Frost burn occurs when your footprints have damaged the plant cells of the frozen grass under the compression of your weight. After the frost has lifted you may see blackened foot impressions over the surface. However, the plant will recover from this naturally.

■ PETS

Dog urine can be an issue at this time of year due to the dormancy of the grass plant. Heavily water the worst affected areas, as soon as possible after the 'offence' has occurred! Tiresome job though!

*Suitable soil – a soil that is in similar quality and texture to the top-soil in which the grass plant is growing. A good place to find a soil of the correct type is in the flower or shrub beds around the perimeter of the lawn.

What to do in

MARCH

■ MOWING

Depending on the ambient soil temperature you may need to commence mowing operations this month. Mow the turf at a high height of cut because you only need to 'tip' off the top part of the leaf.

You should reduce the height of cut slowly over the next three months until reaching your desired level. See page 37 for further information on cutting heights.

■ SEED

Toward the end of this month you should begin to prepare the ground for any spring over-sowing* of grass seed. On smaller lawns, this will mean raking the lawn thoroughly with a spring tine rake before over-sowing, whilst on large lawns, lightly scarifying the lawn is needed before over-sowing. If you are going to establish a completely new lawn from seed, see to pages 13-17.

■ WEEDS

Hand pick any germinating weeds from the lawn. You might consider purchasing a 'daisy grubber' to aid this task from your local DIY store.

■ DISEASE

Look out for signs of disease (see pages 75-79).

■ FROST

Keep off the lawn during periods of frost.

■ EDGES

Establish the lawn edges with a half-moon tool (edging iron) or edging shears as necessary.

*Over-sowing - the application of seed to an established lawn. This maintenance task is vital because throughout the year the lawn will be mown, preventing the grass plant from seeding naturally. The grass plant, as all plants, will have a finite life cycle. Grasses are either annual or perennial (see appendix for explanation) and the seed bank for establishing new growth will periodically need replenishing by over-sowing fresh seed.

What to do in

APRIL

■ COARSE GRASS

Remove any patches of coarse/rough grass infestations by hand, fill the hole with a suitable top-soil, level, firm and over-sow with a desirable grass seed if necessary (see pages 8-11).

■ MOSS

Treat any moss that is growing in the lawn with LAWN SAND. Lawn sand contains sulphate of iron or ferrous sulphate (this kills the moss) and a small amount of nitrogen (N) (usually in the form of ammonium). The ammoniacal nitrogen helps to stimulate growth of the grass plant while the iron (Fe) will kill off and eventually blacken the moss. Ensure the lawn is watered after application. Once the moss is dead, remove it from the lawn with a spring tine rake. For further information on moss and moss control (see pages 87-88).

■ WEEDS

Apply a selective weed-killer to the lawn. A selective weed-killer does not affect the grass plant and there are many available for purchase from most local DIY stores. Always read the label of your chosen type carefully; it must NOT contain the active ingredient 'glyphosate', this chemical will kill off the grass plant. The product purchased should contain active ingredients such as MCPA, Mecoprop-P, 2,4-D. Ensure you read the small print on the back of the label and carefully follow the directions given (see pages 67-74 and 91-92 for further information on weed control).

You can scarify or heavily rake out any dead moss at this time after your March treatment of moss killer.

■ FEED

You may also consider applying a lawn fertiliser towards the middle of this month. Your local DIY store will stock various suitable brands. Look at the ingredients or nutrient ratio on the packet (N, P & K). Try not to purchase one with high levels of Nitrogen (over 36%) because this can encourage excessive leaf growth and will mean you spend a lot of time mowing! Always thoroughly water the lawn after any application of fertiliser. Lawn nutrition is explained in detail on pages 49-54.

■ MOW

Mow the lawn as growth dictates. Remember, the higher the height of cut, the healthier the plant will be.

■ SEED

Over-seed any sparse looking areas of the lawn with a suitable grass seed.

■ AERATE

Aerate the lawn by hand or machine (see pages 55-58). Aerating the lawn will help the soil warm up, encourage growth, allow the soil to drain freely, help break up any compaction that may have occurred over the winter months and generally benefit the health of the lawn.

■ EDGES

Use edging shears to keep the edges of the lawn well trimmed, neat and tidy.

What to do in

MAY

■ MOW

Continue to mow as growth dictates and continue to slowly reduce the cutting height to the desired summer height of cut, if required.

■ WEED

A further application of a suitable selective weed killer may be necessary this month to treat the more persistent weeds. A selective weed-killer does not affect the grass plant and there are many available for purchase from most local DIY stores. Always read the label of your chosen type carefully; it must NOT contain the active ingredient 'glyphosate' because this chemical will kill all plants, including the grass plant. The product purchased should contain active ingredients such as MCPA, Mecoprop-P, 2,4-D, or something similar. Ensure you carefully read the small print on the back of label and follow the direction (see pages 67-73 for further information on weed control).

■ WATER

Water may need to be applied to the lawn this month. Keep an eye on the weather forecast and apply water as necessary (see pages 45-48 for further information).

■ MOSS

Apply another application of LAWN SAND if moss still persists. Lawn Sand contains sulphate of iron or ferrous sulphate (this kills the moss) and a small amount of nitrogen (N) (usually in the form of ammonium). The ammoniacal nitrogen helps to stimulate growth of the grass plant while the iron (Fe) will kill off and eventually blacken the moss. Ensure the lawn is thoroughly watered after application. Once the moss is dead, remove it from the lawn with a spring tine rake. For further information on moss and moss control (see pages 87-88).

■ AERATE

Aerate the lawn if drainage, compaction or thatch is a problem.

■ DISEASE

Check for any signs of disease, especially if you have applied a nitrogenous fertiliser during April.

What to do in

JUNE

■ MOW

According to growth, your summer height of cut should be established now.

■ MOWER

Check and adjust your mowers blades.

■ TOP-DRESS

On high maintenance/ornamental lawns you might consider applying a light top-dressing of a suitable top-soil. This will help maintain a smooth and true surface for mowing and help dilute the lawns thatch layer.

■ WATER

During periods of dry weather irrigate the lawn heavily and infrequently (see pages 45-48 for further information).

■ SCARIFY

If there is a problem with thatch it is still possible to lightly scarify lawns at this time. Ensure that if doing this correct irrigation is applied to the lawn afterward to aid recovery.

■ EDGES

Keep the edges of the lawn trimmed using edging shears

■ WEEDS

Continue to hand weed the lawn. There should be no need to apply a selective weed-killer this month if previously applied.

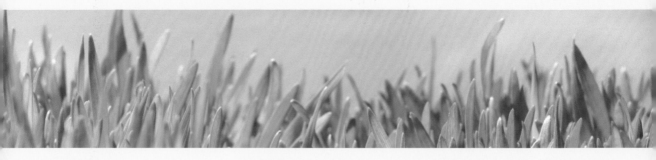

What to do in

JULY

■ MOW

According to growth.

■ FEED

If you lawn is looking weak and thin, you may consider applying a very light dressing of fertiliser but ensure that the nutrient ratios of Nitrogen, Phosphorus & Potassium are low. No more than 10% Nitrogen. Tomato fertiliser is good for this time of year and is very cheap! So is rose fertiliser – you may even consider applying a turf conditioner instead.

■ WATER

During periods of dry weather irrigate the lawn heavily and infrequently (see pages 45-48 for further information).

■ EDGES

Keep the edges of the lawn trimmed using edging shears.

■ WEEDS

Continue to hand weed the lawn each time you mow. If you remove 5-10 weeds each time, before you know it, they may be eradicated completely.

■ AERATE

A light pricking of the soil surface with a hand-fork can be beneficial at this time of year. The demand for oxygen by both the plant and the soil microbes is high. This will also help any applied water drain through the soil quickly and aid thatch breakdown – a worthwhile exercise.

What to do in

AUGUST

■ MOW

According to growth at the summer height of cut (see pages 35-39).

■ WATER

During periods of dry weather irrigate the lawn heavily and infrequently (see pages 45-48 for further information).

■ EDGES

Use edging shears to keep the lawns edges trimmed, neat and tidy.

■ WEEDS

Continue to hand weed the lawn each time you mow.

■ TOP-DRESS

If your lawn is relatively uneven, you may consider applying a light top-dressing at this time. Keep the application light and brush into the sward well.

■ WEED

Remove any weeds by hand.

What to do in

SEPTEMBER

■ MOW

According to growth, towards the end of the month begin to raise the height of cut toward your winter cutting height (see page 37)

■ WATER

During periods of dry weather irrigate the lawn heavily and infrequently (see pages 45-48 for further information).

■ EDGES

Keep the edges of the lawn trimmed using edging shears

■ WEEDS

Continue to hand weed the lawn each time you mow.

■ DISEASE

Look out for any signs of disease (see pages 75-79).

■ MOSS

This month is the best month to treat moss. Treat any moss that is growing in the lawn with LAWN SAND. Lawn Sand contains sulphate of iron or ferrous sulphate (this kills the moss) and a small amount of nitrogen (N) (usually in the form of ammonium). The ammoniacal nitrogen helps to stimulate growth of the grass plant while the iron (Fe) will kill off and eventually blacken the moss. Ensure the lawn is watered after application. Once the moss is dead, remove it from the lawn with a spring tine rake.

■ AERATE

If your lawn has a drainage problem then, towards the end of this month, aerate with suitable equipment or machinery (see pages 55-58 for further information).

■ WORMS

Check for worm activity. Brush off any worm castings with a stiff broom. It is best to wait until the surface is dry before attempting this. Brushing sodden worm castings will only smear the exposed soil into the surface.

■ SEED

Seed any worn areas with suitable grass seed (see pages 10-11). Ensure you do this after the aeration operation, if aerating.

What to do in

OCTOBER

■ MOW

According to growth, at the end of this month you should have your mower set to the winter cutting height (see page 37)

■ WATER

During periods of dry weather irrigate the lawn heavily and infrequently (see pages 45-48 for further information).

■ EDGES

Keep the edges of the lawn trimmed using edging shears

■ WEEDS

Continue to hand weed the lawn each time you mow.

■ DISEASE

Look out for any signs of disease (see pages 75-79).

■ MOSS

Continue to remove the dead or dying moss form the lawn after the September application of lawn sand (see pages 87-90 for further information).

■ AERATE

If you were unable to aerate during September then carry out this operation now (see pages 55-58 for further information).

■ WORMS

Check for worm activity. Brush off any worm castings with a stiff broom. It is best to wait until the surface is dry before attempting this. Brushing sodden worm castings will only smear the exposed soil into the surface.

■ TURF/SEED

You can lay turf at this time and/ or seed any worn areas with suitable grass seed (see pages 13-17 for further information).

■ DEBRIS

Remove any falling leaves or debris from the lawn.

■ BRUSH

Brush the lawn with a stiff broom twice this month. Carry out this operation before mowing because the mower will then pick up or mulch any debris.

■ FEED

It is a good idea to apply an iron-based fertiliser product to the lawn at this time. This will toughen up the sward and give some winter colour to the lawn. Do not be tempted to apply a strong fertiliser at this time because it may encourage disease over the winter.

What to do in

NOVEMBER

■ MOW

Only mow if growth dictates.

■ EQUIPMENT

Oil and maintain all of your lawn care equipment. Place all equipment in a suitable, dry storage area for over-wintering.

■ DEBRIS

Continue to remove any fallen debris appearing on the lawn.

■ FROST

If frost is present keep off the lawn.

■ DISEASE

Look out for signs of disease (see pages 75-80).

■ TURF

It is possible to lay turf at this time (see pages 13-17).

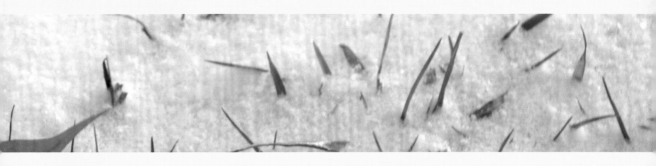

What to do in

DECEMBER

■ READ

Put your feet up and read your Lawn Guide thoroughly.

■ LOOK

Keep a close eye on how shade effects your lawn. Note the cause and improve if possible, either right away or later in the new year. Improving the available light levels on your lawn will help encourage stronger growth during the warmer months.

■ EQUIPMENT

Oil and maintain all of your lawn care equipment.

■ DEBRIS

Continue to remove any fallen debris appearing on the lawn.

■ FROST

If frost is present keep off the lawn.

■ DISEASE

Look out for signs of disease (see pages 75-80).

■ AERATE

Lightly aerate the lawn with a fork or solid tines if the soil is not too wet. This will aid winter surface drainage from any heavy or prolonged rainfall.

MOWING

Mowing can be described as a defoliation process that prevents the grass developing to its maximum potential!

The response of grass to mowing is simply to grow more! It is the most frequently carried out maintenance operation and, depending upon the mower you use, or choose, can either be a very enjoyable operation or a chore that you do not look forward to carrying out. It may come as a surprise, but your system of mowing can actually kill off some types of grasses while stimulating others.

It is well known that infrequently cut lawns will nurse and develop undesirable grasses which, eventually, may over-run the more desirable species. Mowing should be carried out as a regular maintenance operation, unless the grass is purposely planted to cover an out-of-site rough area. Good domestic lawns should be cared for and mown on a regular basis because this is the only way to guarantee good results.

Types of mower

Mowers cut grass in two different ways. A cylinder mower traps the grass between two blades (one fixed – called the bottom blade), while a rotary mower cuts by rotating a solid metal or plastic blade/s parallel to the grass. Generally, cylinder mowers give a better quality cut and finish to the lawn, although modern rotary mowers can also produce a good quality of finish. However, if you want to

FIG. 7 – STRIPING IS EASY ON A HEALTHY LAWN!

FIG. 8 – AN UN-MOWN, UNCARED FOR FRONT LAWN

mow at very low cutting heights then a cylinder mower will need to be purchased and, if you want a striping effect to appear on your lawn after mowing, you will need to purchase a mower (either cylinder or rotary) with a rear roller fitted.

Mowers, be they cylinder or rotary, are powered by various means – petrol engines, electric motor (mains operated), some rotary mowers operate on a cushion of air and some cylinder mowers are driven by manual pushing. Another popular way to cut grass is with cord cutters. These operate on the same principle as a rotary cutter, but instead a thin piece or pieces of plastic cord rotate at high speed to provide the cutter. These are usually powered electrically. If you are wondering which type of mower suits your particular situation there are a number of things to take into consideration.

What type should I buy?
Major considerations when purchasing a new mower

a) The size and type of your lawn/s and the space available for maintenance and storage

b) The initial purchase price and the expected life span of the machine

c) Does it have the ability to collect grass clippings – if so what quantity and how easy or difficult is the bin to put on and take off?

d) Ease of starting, how it feels to handle and its servicing requirements

e) Roller type (if present)

f) Do you have banks that need mowing? – if so, can the machine cope with these?

g) Cost and availability of spares

h) Length of flex for electrically powered machines

Type of mower	Suitable for
Cylinder	Fine ornamental and leisure lawns
Rotary	Leisure and utility, rough grasses and verges
Cord	Lawn edges, bases or walls, trees & around washing lines.

TABLE 8 – TYPES OF MOWER

Other considerations

High quality finish required? – To achieve this purchase a cylinder mower with 8 – 10 blades on the cylinder. These will produce the desired number of cuts per metre for a quality finish. This type of mower is not recommended for infrequently cut lawns.

Clipping - collection or not? – to produce fine looking lawns some type of grass collection system will be needed to produce the polished finish required. The downside to this is that lawns that have the clippings collected while mowing may need more frequent applications of fertiliser This is because, clippings returned to the lawn after mowing, fertilise the soil through their recycled nutrients ($\frac{1}{3}$ of annually required Nitrogen (N)) when broken down by soil fungus and bacteria.

Area – if your lawn is over 1000 m2 then it is advisable to purchase a petrol engine mower

Stripes – To produce stripes the mower will need to have a sturdy rear roller fitted

Infrequently cut lawns – Purchase a petrol/electric driven rotary mower

Don't like walking? – Purchase a ride on rotary mower

Least amount of physical exertion! – Purchase either a ride-on or petrol driven mower.

Adjusting the height of cut – The easier this is to do the better. Check how the height is adjusted and the range of heights available. For quality ornamental lawns then the mower should be capable of being adjusted down to around 5 mm as some ornamental lawns are cut as low as 5 or 6 mm.

How to cut the grass

Grass should be mown a little at a time with the aim of removing a third of the available leaf every time you mow. A cut of one-third allows the grass adequate time to recover from the cut because the majority of the leaf is left intact. The leaf is an extremely important part of the plant as it is the area where photosynthesis takes place. Photosynthesis is the way the grass turns simple compounds such as water into food for growth. If you take two thirds or more of the leaf away during mowing the grass plant may become susceptible to disease attack, can exhibit a yellow colour, become weak and thin in growth, thereby allowing weeds and undesirable grasses to encroach and compete for space.

When to mow

Table 9 provides suggested mowing schedules for different lawns. However, it should be noted that ideally you will mow according to growth. If the aim is to achieve a smooth, low cut, dense lawn (similar of that to a golf putting green) then the mowing operation should be carried out every single day throughout the growing season.

Mowing when the surface is dry will not only be easier for the operator, but will also prevent the mower blocking so giving a cleaner, more professional finish to the surface. In essence, mowing should be done when the grass demands and the weather allows.

During the winter the height of cut of the mower should be raised (see Table 9) to help the grass develop a good, deep, root system that will help the lawn combat any wear received. Shading of the lawn can also be a problem to growth, so keeping the cut high will also assist with the maintenance of the quality of the lawn.

Collection of clippings

The professional groundsman or greenkeeper refers to this as 'boxing

HEIGHT AND FREQUENCY OF CUTTING			
Lawn type	Height of cut summer	Height of cut winter	Frequency of cutting per week
Ornamental	5 – 10 mm	12 – 18 mm	Mow every two or three days – depending upon growth
Leisure	15 – 20 mm	20 – 25 mm	Mow every three or four days – depending upon growth
Utility	25 mm	25 mm +	Mow every six or seven days – depending upon growth

TABLE 9 – RECOMMENDED HEIGHTS OF CUT

GRASS CLIPPING CAN MOUNT UP! (PICTURE COURTESY OF LEE JACKSON MCFC)

off' the clippings. The choice to remove or return the clippings will depend upon the gardeners preference. The relative advantages and disadvantages are listed below:

Removing clippings

- Gives a cleaner looking finish
- Removes all leaf litter from the surface
- Removes weed seeds
- Discourages worms
- Can reduce the incidence of disease

Returning clippings

- Can encourage worm activity
- Grass will keep a better winter and summer colour
- Reduces the need to fertilise (environmentally friendly)

- Can encourage yellow patches if thickly covering the turf underneath
- Can encourage the incidence of disease
- Can spread weed and moss seeds
- Encourages softer grass growth that can be less tolerant to wear

The direction of cutting

If the size of lawn allows it, mowing in different directions should be carried out every time the lawn is cut. If your mower has a roller, mowing in different directions will not only help the grass grow upright but will also prevent any 'nap' or grain occurring in the lawn. Nap is where the grass grows flat making it more difficult to create attractive stripes on the lawn. Areas of flat growth will also encourage the development of thatch in the lawn. Thatch is an undesirable

layer of dead and dying organic matter found at the base of the plant, but on top of the soils surface. Thatch is explained more fully on page 59.

How to mow in a straight line

Mowing a straight line on a lawn is not as simple as most people think. The key to perfect lines is knowing the cutting width of your machine. Mowers are generally always wider in body than they cut. Look at the width of the cylinder or the rotary blade underneath the main housing and clearly mark with tape on the top of the machine the width of the cutting mechanism. Once you know this and can clearly see it as you look down at the mower, the mowing operation becomes more straightforward and a professional finish is easier to create.

As previously mentioned it is the rollers on the mower that create the stripe patterns. Rollers lay the grass down and it is the light reflecting off this flat grass that gives the effect of light and dark green. When mowing a lawn you should always mow against what you see as the dark stripe. Once turned at the opposite end of the run, again, as you look back down the line you had just mowed, you will see it as a dark stripe, you should then use this as a guide for mowing the next line.

The best looking stripes are achieved from mastering three things which are (a) that the very first stripe mown is perfectly straight; (b) that you know the exact cutting width of your mower; and, (c) that you concentrate when returning down the next run and closely follow the previously made stripe.

The first stripe can be made to be straight through using a focal point in the distance. This focal point should be above the level of the ground, preferably at eye level and when ready to mow you should walk toward it keeping your eye on it all the time. When returning along the previously cut line, focus about 1 or 2 metres in front of you concentrating on the edge of the cut area. Occasionally, you should look down at the width marks on the mower to check you are neither crossing

the mown mark by too much (2 – 4 centimetres is enough) nor too little. With practice you will have straight lines in no time at all!

Why grass looks stripy!

As a mower rolls over the lawn it will lay the grass down and it is this laying down grass that gives a pattern when cutting. Grass lying toward you will give a dark green effect while grass lying away from you will give a light green colour. The pattern will remain in the lawn for some time after mowing – the exact length of time will vary and is determined by the amount of growth and on the density of the lawn. You do not only have to focus on stripes, many other patterns can be created and arranged

in some very attractive designs. (See Figs 9 and 10)

Mowing problems

The task of mowing can bring its own problems.

WASH BOARDING – This describes a series of mounds formed on the surface of the soil that run across and along the mowing lines. Wash boarding appears as a wave-like pattern and is caused by consistent mowing in the same direction which, over time, produces a ripple effect in the soil surface. This can be a particular problem if the lawn is mown with a ride on cylinder mower.

FIG. 9 – TARTAN STRIPING PATTERN (PICTURE COURTESY OF LEE JACKSON MCFC)

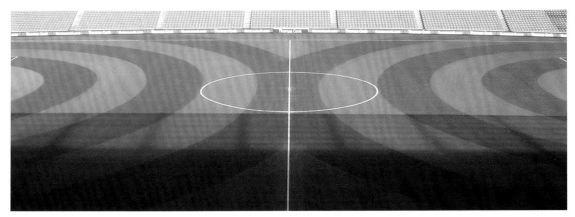

FIG. 10 – STRIPES DON'T NEED TO BE STRAIGHT! (PICTURE COURTESY OF LEE JACKSON MCFC)

FIG. 11 - SCALPING – GRASS RECOVERING AFTER

FIG. 12 - BROWN TIPPING – THE TIP OF THE GRASS PLANT TURNS BROWN AND DIES OFF

Remedy

- Change direction of mowing frequently.
  Manually work a light top-dressing of the surface of the lawn (in ridges only).

RIBBING – This is generally caused when the grass too long, is wet or the mower is badly adjusted. Ribbing is a series of narrow bands of long, then short, cut grass running across and along the mown strip. Ribbing can be caused by a cylinder mower with the blades revolving too slowly or because the number of blades on the cylinder is insufficient for the quality of cut and the cutting height desired.

Remedy

- Cut the lawn more frequently
- Cutting height is too low for the cylinder to cope with the length of grass encountered – raise the cutting height
- The grass is too wet and is jamming the cylinder – mow when dry
- Insufficient number of cutting blades – purchase a machine with greater number of blades

SCALPING – This occurs where the surface is uneven and bumpy leading to the mower cutting the grass on the ridges excessively low. The scalped grass loses all its leaf and therefore colour. See Figure 11.

Remedy

- Raise the cutting height and improve surface levels by frequent top-dressing
- Do not press downward or put excess weight on the mowers handles
- Thatch levels are too great – reduce thatch through scarification

HOVER SCALPING – The tips of leaves browning off after mowing is a particular problem on lawns with ryegrass in them and where the mower blades are blunt or dull.

Caused by:

a) Dull blades – sharpen or replace
b) Damaged blades and/or damaged bottom blade of cylinder mower – Check machine condition and repair if necessary
c) Cutting when wet – only mow the lawn when it is dry

EDGING THE LAWN

Many lawns will have areas within them laid to paths, have borders surrounding or within them and will meet walls or fences or other building work. The edges may be raised high or low – *these in themselves can lead to tripping hazards if not carefully managed and constructed* – in fact; any lawn edge, left long enough without the correct management, can distract the eye and look aesthetically un-pleasing. Maintenance of these areas can be made to be quick, efficient and easy on the operator or the complete opposite!

The tools selected to maintain edges should be chosen carefully and be the correct type for the job at hand. A well trimmed, neat and unbroken edge will give the entire lawn area a cared-for, manicured look that accentuates the overall condition of the lawn.

Edging tips and advice

A simple row of paving slabs layed next to a fence or wall in place of a flower bed will give a neat and easy to maintain finish to the edge or end of a lawn. If the paving is laid to be slightly below the level of the lawn, edging will be easier to carry out on a frequent basis.

Metal or wooden strips can be laid out around the edge of a raised lawn can help contain excess growth, but these can be easily damaged so should be installed firmly and correctly to prevent further future repair work

If you have a tree or trees in the lawn that are grassed underneath, it can be beneficial for both tree and grass if a collar is cut around the base of the tree (can vary in diameter from 0.5 – 2 metres). This prevents the grasses directly under the tree from dying or thinning due to the shade caused by the tree's canopy. It will also prevent competition between grass and tree for water and nutrients and prevent the tree being damaged by mowing or maintenance operations. When this collar is edged properly, it will also accentuate the tree and help make it a feature of the garden.

The tools required

There is quite a range of equipment available for trimming the edge of lawns. This choice can be narrowed down by understanding the type of edges you have on your lawn and thinking about the quality of finish you desire.

The simplest form of lawn edger is the spade. By walking along the edge of the lawn and chipping away the grass and a slither of soil it is possible to create an edge, although this edge is unlikely to be uniform unless extreme care is taken. This method will also (over a period of years) reduce the size of the lawn because on each occasion soil is being removed at the edge.

HALF MOON – this is a simple half-circular metal blade mounted on a handle that is used to remove soil and grass from the edge of a lawn to create a new clean edge or re-establish a worn one. The half-moon is a popular tool within professional greenkeeping as it is easy to use and very agile. Again, the half moon will remove soil and, therefore, eventually reduce the size of the lawn.

POWERED EDGERS – Can be pushed by hand and also motor driven. Care should be taken with these as mistakes can be hard to fix. Both tend to produce a good quality of finish but can remove soil when being used.

STRIMMERS AND ELECTRIC TRIMMER – Many types are available. Although these machines are easy and quick to use extra care should be taken with them as the high speed spinning nylon cord will throw up a lot of dust and small stones. These machines must be used with great care as the slightest mistake will lead to loss of grass or damage to the edge. It is advised to use eye (protective glasses), arm (jumper) and leg (trousers) protection when using these.

EDGING SHEARS – Long-handled edging shears or border shears are a very useful tool to maintain lawn edges. When carefully used they will remove grass only, allowing the edges to establish themselves and become tougher to wear and tear. They are easy to use and cheap to buy. Care should be taken to keep the shears' blade edges sharp for the best results.

HAND SHEARS – These should be considered as a general purpose implement rather than specific lawn edgers. They are suitable for cutting lawn edges although can be cumbersome and time consuming to use for this purpose. There are specific single-handed grass shears for sale at many garden centres. These can be a useful tool for the perfectionist for finishing the edges after cutting with a more substantial edger has been carried out. To cut most lawn edges with these alone would be a time consuming and tiring operation.

WATERING THE LAWN

During a typical year most lawns will be perfectly able to survive without irrigation for about eight months, however, during dry periods it may be necessary to apply water to the turf. The turfgrass plant consists of over 85% water (the rest being dry matter) so it is clear that water is vital for turf grass growth and development.

When we irrigate grasses we don't actually water the plant itself but the aim is to replenish the water in the soil because it is from here the roots obtain the water required by the plant. During periods of drought the water reserves in the soil are depleted eventually leading to plant wilt. In such circumstances irrigation will become essential. If the lawn has been well cared for throughout the year, with good husbandry as outlined in this book, then the root system should be both extensive and deep enabling the plant to survive for long periods without the need for supplementary irrigation.

Why irrigate?

There are many valid reasons why we should or should not irrigate soils. Excessive applications of irrigation water can and will lead to as many troubles as insufficient irrigation. We should consider applying water to the soil for the following reasons:

- Irrigation keeps the plant alive
- Irrigation maintains turf grass colour, appearance and strength
- Irrigation is vital for the germination process of seeds
- Water moving through the plant cools it during hot periods
- Irrigation prevents turf disorders such as dry areas or dry patch development

- Irrigation pushes fertiliser granules into the turf and water is vital for converting the fertiliser into forms that are available for plant uptake
- Water is a vital constituent of photosynthesis (the process that allows the grass plant to grow, develop and recover from wear).

When to water

A lawn will need watering when the effects of drought can be visually seen on the surface. Initially, the colour of the grass may become dull, brown or take on a distinct 'bluish' tint.

When walking on the lawn footprints persist for longer as the

FIG. 13 – DROUGHTED LAWN

FIG. 14 - SEVERE DROUGHT LEADS TO SOIL CRACKING

grass is unable to upright itself due to the lack of water in its cells. Eventually, the leaves turn brown and begin to shrivel and the roots will dry up and ultimately die. You should irrigate the lawn when you notice the first of these signs.

How much water to apply

The speed with which water stress symptoms appear will largely depend upon the soil type the grass is growing upon. Sandy soils hold less water and quickly lose more water than heavier clay soils. Subsequently, grasses growing upon sandy soils will exhibit water stress signs earlier. Under hot, dry and windy weather conditions, soils can lose up to and over 25mm of water in 7 days. The amount of water required to replace this would equate to 27 litres of water per square metre.

Although professional groundsmen and greenkeepers can measure and irrigate to moisture loss from the soil with the aid of a weather station and soil moisture probes, it is not practical, or strictly feasible, for home owners to do this and therefore informed judgement will be needed for when to apply water to your lawn.

As a general rule, heavy and infrequent applications of water will be better for your lawn and the grasses growing within it. This type of ethos encourages deep and extensive roots, discourages disease and aids overall plant health. The alternate to this is light and frequent watering but this will encourage thatch build up, diseases and prevent a strong, deep, drought resistant root system developing. The aim of watering is to aid the plant in developing a strong, deep root system by periodically restoring

the soil water reserves to their full water-holding capacity. This can only be achieved with heavy infrequent applications. Basically, heavy, infrequent applications encourage and stimulate the plant to build an extensive root system through encouraging the roots down into the soil. Light and infrequent applications encourage the roots to stay near the surface.

Whilst grass roots require relatively high amounts of water a slight deficiency is not always a bad thing. Some degree of stress on the plant will benefit the root system. If the soil surface is periodically allowed dry out, entry of oxygen into the soil can be permitted aiding growth. This dry surface encourages deeper root growth leading to a more drought resistant plant.

We can summarise by stating:

a) Little and often applications of water result in uneven wetting of the soil and lead to a shallow root system. Water applications of this frequency can lead (during the drier months) to the condition where any water applied will simply be lost to the atmosphere the very next day through 'evapotranspiration' (water lost from the leaf and the soil) leaving a dry uninviting under-lying soil.

b) Infrequent, heavy applications of water at intervals with a number of days between (say 7 to 10 days) supplemented by lighter applications during every third day. This encourages air into the soil profile and a deep extensive root system., while at the same time providing a supply of water deeper in the soil profile lessening the risk of water loss through evaporation.

c) Lastly, when a soil is very dry it will accept water very slowly and, if a lot of water is applied quickly, most of this will simply run across the surface and off the lawn. The most efficient method to wet a dry soil is to lightly wet the lawn initially and give this time to work its way into the surface before applying the bulk of the water. This ensures that when applying the main supply, it percolates into the soil more efficiently and leads to less waste.

What to water with?

There is a vast array of watering equipment that can be used or installed for the purposes of applying water to a lawn. The simplest and cheapest, but most laborious method is using a watering can and the most sophisticated and expensive is an installed automatic system. The method chosen will be dependant upon your budget, the size of the lawn and, of course, user preference. For me, on small to medium size lawns, a high-quality hose fitted with a good rose produces the best results providing you have good water pressure at the tap. However, the other popular methods are detailed below:

WATERING CANS – Not really acceptable, except for extremely small grassed areas.

HOSE PIPES – Can be used for small to medium sized lawns and (so long as the operator works evenly and effectively) are particularly good at ensuring the entire surface gets a good covering of water. With a rose fitted on the end the spray can be adjusted to put out either fine or heavy droplets of water.

PERFORATED TUBING – Not really suitable for watering lawned areas. Good for watering flower beds and such-like.

SPRINKLERS – Can be static, underground pop-ups, portable rotary arm, travelling rotary arm or oscillating. Used to cover large areas of ground with minimal human in-put. The most effective system for applying water is the static, installed pop-up system because this ensures an even coverage, is generally easy to operate but, it is the most expensive. It is advised that you hire professional fitters to install such a system because there are a number of calculations to be made before installation can proceed.

Most home owners will purchase one of the portable rotary arm types of sprinkler or an oscillating sprinkler. These are easy to set up and operate and, if necessary, can be moved quickly to water another part of the lawn. When using this type you must ensure that all areas of the lawn receive equal amounts of water as it is easy to forget about these once set in motion!

FEEDING THE LAWN

All plants (including the grass plant) require periodic feeding to be at their best. The nutrition programme you use to feed your lawn will, in the long term, affect not only its colour and appearance, but also its tolerance to wear, its disease resistance, its density and its ability to grow effectively. Failure to feed correctly can lead to an impoverished looking yellow and weak lawn, full of undesirable plant species such as weeds. But, before we really look into effective feeding we need to understand that some grasses, such as the fine-leaved fescues, actually require very little in the way of fertiliser and will develop actively under a very light feeding programme. No more than one light application of complete fertiliser per year will be needed. However, if you have a lawn with a high percentage of either rye grasses (Lolium species) or bent grasses (Agrostis species) then

Soil type	Suggested frequency for fertiliser application
Very Sandy	Two to four light applications. May also need micro nutrient applications (rare)
Silt loam	One or two light applications
Clay loam	One or two light applications
Organic	One or two light applications

TABLE 10 – APPLICATION RATES VERSUS SOIL TYPE

more frequent applications may be required.

The main foods required by grasses are nitrogen (N), phosphorus (P) and potassium (K) and depending on the soil type you have there may be a need to periodically apply other nutrients to the lawn. See Tables 10 (above) and 11.

Further guidance is given below;

Spring feeding

For most lawns one application of a complete fertiliser dressing should be adequate per year. This can be applied either as a spring dressing or, alternatively, as an autumn dressing. Lawns that receive high levels of wear throughout the year may benefit from more frequent applications of fertiliser (spring and autumn) if they

continue to look worn, weakened and damaged.

The spring dressing should be applied to the lawn once the grass looks like it is becoming active and growing after the winter period. You should not apply fertiliser too early in the spring because this may encourage disease to develop. Also, make sure the plants are growing actively because if they aren't they will not be able to make use of the applied fertiliser.

An alternate to spring feeding (if you are to apply the complete dressing during the autumn) is to apply lawn sand. Lawn sand has the advantage of acting like a weed and moss killer as well as a fertiliser. It consists of a sulphate iron mixed with sand and will give a deep green colour to the

Nutrient	Effect	Typical sources of nutrient	Percentage nutrient
Nitrogen (N)	Improves leaf growth, colour, aids recovery from wear, improves sward density, can increase disease proneness due to thinning of cell walls	Ammonium sulphate Ammonium nitrate Potassium nitrate Isobutylidene (IBDU) Urea formaldehyde (UF) Sodium nitrate Potassium nitrate Hoof & horn Dried blood	21% 35% 13% 32% Approx. 40% 16% 15% 13% 10-14%
Phosphorus (P)	Aids establishment, seed-head production and reproduction, involved in the maturation process of the plant	Superphosphate Triplesuperphosphate Ammonium phosphate Bone meal	19% 47% 50% 22%
Potassium (K)	Aids rooting, increases drought hardiness, improves disease resistance, aids the retention of water	Potassium chloride Potassium sulphate	60% 50%
Calcium (Ca)	Important for the cell walls, needed for cell production and growth, can neutralise potentially toxic substances within the plant cells	Rarely becomes unavailable due to the high quantities available	
Magnesium (Mg)	Important for colour, needed for the movement of phosphorus within the plant, involved with many enzymes within the plant	Magnesium sulphate Kieserite Dolomitic limestone Epsom salts	10% 27% 11% 17%
Sulphur (S)	Primarily involved in production of amino acids needed to produce protein	Only in extreme cases would this need to be applied as a single nutrient	
Iron (Fe)	Needed for colour, helps make nitrogen available. Too much in the soil will reduce levels of available phosphorus	Ferrous sulphate Ferrous oxalate Chelated iron	20% 30%

TABLE II – FERTILISER TYPES, EFFECTS AND SOURCES

lawn after application. Some high quality ornamental lawns may receive a number of applications of lawn sand through the year to maintain colour and appearance, whilst killing off any germinated weeds. It is advised that after applying a lawn sand (as with all fertilisers) that the lawn is irrigated thoroughly.

Autumn feeding

If a spring fertiliser was applied there will be no need to apply an autumn dressing unless the sward is looking particularly weak and thin. Examine the sward mid august to determine the need.

Summer feeding

Nitrogen is required throughout the entire growing season by the plant and it is this nutrient that forms the basis of summer feeding. It is only recommended to apply nitrogenous fertilisers during the summer period if you wish to improve the density of the lawn. If colour is required then it is recommended that lawn sand is applied. Note that excessive applications of nitrogenous fertiliser throughout the year will lead to excessive thatch build up, poor wear tolerance and increase the possibility of disease.

What fertilisers do

Table 12 briefly gives the role of each major nutrient within the grass plant. Using this information we can begin to understand the effects that these may have on the plant after application and therefore modify what we apply.

One way of determining if fertilisers need to be applied is to closely inspect the plant looking for what are known as deficiency symptoms. If spotted (should be a rare occurrence) these symptoms can give a clear picture as to what type of fertiliser should be added.

FIG. 15 – NUTRIENT STARVED GRASS

Nutrient	Deficiency symptom
Nitrogen (N)	Yellowing of older leaves on plant. Closely followed by yellowing of entire plant and slow growth.
Phosphorus (P)	Older leaves turn dark green followed closely by a purple discolouration of the leaf edges
Potassium (K)	Leaf tips tend to turn brown and dry up while leaf edges look burnt and brown. You may find excessive amounts of new growth appearing from the plant
Calcium (Ca)	Very rare, but if present the youngest leaves turn a red-brown colour at their edges. This colour likely to turn light red as the deficiency persists
Magnesium (Mg)	Older leaves exhibit a cherry-red discolouration. Necrosis of the leaves appears as the deficiency persists
Sulphur (S)	Very rare, but if present leaves initially turn a pale yellow while the leaf tip and edges turn brown and appear burnt.
Iron (Fe)	Interveinal yellowing of the leaf appears. Growth of the plant can be slowed significantly
Chlorine (Cl)	Not yet determined
Molybdenum (Mo)	Interveinal yellowing that appears initially in older leaves. Followed by necrosis and withering
Copper (Cu)	A bluish discolouration of leaf tips. Eventually leading to leaf death
Zinc (Zn)	Stunted leaf growth with thin and dishevelled leaves
Manganese (Mn)	Interveinal chlorosis that soon has small yellow dead spots appearing. Leaf eventually withers
Boron (B)	Symptoms take a long time to appear. Stunted rosette type growth appears followed by interveinal chlorotic streaking.

TABLE 12 – NUTRIENT DEFICIENCY SYMPTOMS

INTERVEINAL = between the leaf veins running up the leaf

CHLOROSIS = Yellowing of the leaf (can be partial)

NECROSIS = Browning and death to some parts or all of the leaf

Many fertilisers are available on the market and come in many different forms. The following table introduces the most popular.

What type of fertiliser should I apply?

Tables 11 and 13 provide a host of information on fertilisers. Why do you need to know all this? Well, anyone who manages turf should understand what the differences in fertilisers are and what effects they may have on the plant.

If you feel unsure as to when and what type of fertiliser to apply, then as a general guide apply a N P K fertiliser early spring, apply a light Nitrogenous fertiliser during the summer and then, a final application of N & K only. Preferably, this should be during the early Autumn.

Please note the above is intended as a guide only. Fertiliser applications will differ for soil type, grass species, time of year, weather conditions, ambient soil temperature, soil moisture levels, soil compactions levels and so on. At the end of the day, there is no real right or wrong as every turf area is essentially different. However, by reading, understanding and utilising the knowledge available in this book you will be informed enough to make the right decisions for your particular situation and goals.

Form of fertiliser (Should be written somewhere on the bag or container)	Comment
Organic fertiliser	Would have once been living - since processed to make fertilser
Inorganic fertiliser	Made of synthetic material(s)
Elemental or element	One chemical, an example being a fertiliser containing only a source of nitrogen
Compound	A mixture of more than one element
Quick release	Nutrient released over a short period of time
Slow release	Nutrient released over a long period of time (usually 3 – 6 months)
Controlled release	Nutrient released in a controlled manner generally over a long period of time. Control can be through temperature or level of wetness
Granular	Elements compressed into granules for ease of distribution over large areas
Chelated fertilisers	Trace elements when applied as straights are often in chelated form: these are organic molecules surrounding the inorganic molecule preventing it from becoming immobilised in the soil
Mini granular	Elements compressed into small granules for ease of distribution and to reduce amount picked up through mowing
Powder	Element(s) applied as a powder. Not an accurate method and usually quick release
Liquid	Element(s) dissolved in water. Easy application and usually a quick response seen. There is a growing demand for liquid fertilisers they may be sprayed onto the turf surface or injected into the soil, both compound and straight are available.

TABLE 13 – FORMS OF FERTILISER

Applying fertiliser

There are two methods with which we can apply fertiliser to a lawn. The first is by hand and the second mechanically via a spreader.

HAND APPLICATION – Not recommended unless the person applying has experience. There is a high risk of over and under application when applying fertiliser by hand. It is recognised as being difficult to evenly apply the feed when applying fertiliser this way. If you must apply fertiliser by hand then divide the lawn up into strips to walk along while applying the feed. For extra safety, mark strips across the width of the lawn as well, divide the total application rate in half and apply in both directions.

MECHANICAL – The bulk of fertilisers applied to soil or turf are done so using a fertiliser spreader (distributor). Distributors must be capable of applying a wide range of fertiliser forms from powder to granular and there should be some way of adjusting the application rate. All parts of the distributor should, ideally, be made of materials resistant to rust as fertilisers rust metals quickly. Also, the distributor should be capable of being adapted to allow spreading of grass seed and top-dressing as and when necessary. The distributor usually consists of a hopper mounted on wheels. The fertiliser may be thrown out from a spinning disc through centrifugal force or dropped from a moving belt directly onto the lawn surface.

Whichever mechanical device is used, it must be set or calibrated correctly before applying the fertiliser. Care is needed to prevent too much overlap and ideally the fertiliser should be spread in two different directions to ensure even application.

Preparing the lawn for fertilising

Prior to applying either the spring or autumn fertilisers the lawn should have been spiked, slit or scarified to provide openings through the grass plants and into the soil (if you are following the recommended programme this book outlines these tasks would have already been carried out). It is the openings in the turf

FIG. 16 – FERTILISER GRANULES ON SOIL SURFACE

that allow the fertiliser to ingress through the grass and thatch layers through to the soil profile and from here the nutrient can be converted efficiently into forms available for plant uptake. Fertiliser left on the surface will encourage surface rooting and may present a risk of grass burn. If the soil is very hard or dry it should be well irrigated before applying the fertiliser. It is recommended that the lawn is watered immediately after the application of any fertiliser.

Characteristics	Quick release	Slow release
Plant growth response	Rapid plant response, flushes of growth sometimes occur	Initially a slow response but a uniform growth will occur over a long period of time
Length of time before plant response	Short (days or weeks)	Long (weeks to months, dependant upon coating used)
Application	Most forms	Dry forms
Potential to burn plant	Potentially high risk	Low risk
Cost	Relatively inexpensive	Expensive
Example	Ammonium nitrate, urea, ammonium sulphate	IBDU, Urea Formaldehyde

TABLE 14 – QUICK RELEASE VERSUS SLOW RELEASE

AERATION

Introduction

Aeration is perhaps the most underused and undervalued maintenance operation in lawn care.

During the year a lawn will be trampled by feet and have various machines and pieces of equipment pulled across and over it. When the soil is wet even the weight of the operator walking while mowing the lawn will begin to compact soil. Consequently, many lawns deteriorate due to the effects of soil compaction and, if the lawn is also mis-managed, it will deteriorate further due to the effects and consequences of excess thatch. Aeration is the term used to describe the mechanical methods used to combat the effects of excessive thatch and/or soil compaction.

Soil compaction can be described as the soil particles being squashed together leaving minute spaces or pores between them. The end result is little or no room for root development and growth and reduced levels of oxygen held in the soil that is so vital for initiating root

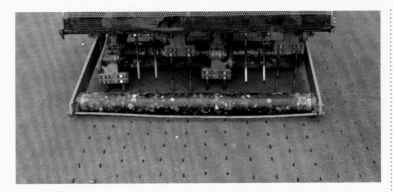

FIG. 17 – THE AFTER EFFECTS OF VERTI-DRAINING A GRASS SURFACE
PICTURE COURTESY - CH GROUNDS MAINTENANCE LTD WWW.CHGROUNDS.COM

growth and general plant health. Small pores tend to hold water very strongly making the soil prone to wetness whilst large pore spaces easily give up the water to the plant root and allow rapid drainage to occur. Aeration is a task that should be carried out not to calendar dates but whenever necessary. It will not only encourage and aid the growth of a dense, healthy turf but also aid the grasses resistance to diseases, water logging, weed and pest infestations.

Topsoil is intrinsically susceptible to compaction, especially when consisting of clay, silt or if organic by nature. The reason is that these soil types have extremely small mineral

particles within them that are easily squashed to form hard, impenetrable barriers. If your lawn is hard and suffers from holding water on its surface for a long time then it is probably suffering from localised or complete compaction. Compaction will eventually lead to a stressed grass plant that cannot grow to its fullest potential. Most compaction occurring in any soil is likely to develop in the top one or two inches of the profile.

The task of aeration is to break open the soil and lift it to promote breaking up of the compact surface. Water can then drain through easily, oxygen can enter and undesirable, root inhibiting gases such as carbon dioxide and hydrogen sulphide can escape easily.

When to aerate

Though most lawns may not require annual aeration of the entire surface the benefits of the operation can bring fantastic results if carried out correctly. Those aspiring to have an ornamental lawn of the highest quality or those with lawns that suffer excessive wear and tear should read this section with interest and carry out the procedure on a regular yearly basis.

Aeration benefits the lawn by:

a) Preventing loss of water from the soil surface and allowing more to percolate into the soil.

b) Increasing the rooting depth of the plant thereby improving drought resistance

c) Breaks down hard undesirable layers within the soil that can prevent root development

d) Increasing the levels of beneficial fungi and bacteria in the soil

e) Increasing the rates at which thatch is broken down

f) Helping fertiliser and water to easily work their way into the soil profile

g) Cutting through stems, stolons and rhizomes will increase new shoot and root growth

Types of aerating equipment

There are three main types of tines used for aerating lawns. The slit tine is used to severe roots and stolons to encourage and stimulate root and shoot growth, break through layers of thatch to hasten decomposition, allow water to penetrate the surface and improve the soils rate of gaseous exchange.

The solid tine has the same effect as the slit tine although it has more value and use on hard, very compacted areas.

The third type is the hollow tine. The hollow tine will relieve compaction through removing a core of soil and grass from the lawn. It is especially useful where drainage has been a problem and you would like to incorporate sandier material into the soil because the hole created is an ideal site for accepting top-dressing materials.

Each type of tine is normally fitted onto a fork or other type of hand held implement although some larger garden centres may stock self propelled machines for the task. When aerating by hand the work is rather laborious and can be tiring, however, aerating is essential for healthy strong turf growth and development.

Before commencing any aeration procedure you should check the underlying condition of the soil. A soil that is too hard may damage the machine or implement used and may even lead to personal injury for the operator carrying out the task. While a very wet soil can effectively render the operation useless! When a soil is too wet the spikes penetrating the soil simply push it down and out smearing the edges of the hole. This will not relieve any compaction and can worsen an already bad situation. Ideally, the soil should be in a dryish

FIG. 18 - COMPACTED SOIL LEADS TO GRASS LOSS

FIG. 19 – THE AFTER EFFECTS OF FORKING

state but wet enough to allow the tine or spike to penetrate the soil.

Aeration and compaction relief

There is a distinct difference between aerating a soil and relieving compaction. A slit tine spiker, solid tine spiker or similar can only aerate the soil. The spike or solid tine on these machines simply goes in and out. This allows gaseous exchange to occur between soil profile and the atmosphere above. Gases such as oxygen can enter while the undesirable types can escape. Slit or solid tining will NOT relieve compaction as there is no soil lifting created by the operation.

To relieve compaction the surface will require lifting. If the soil has

been squashed down together, then it seems natural to relieve this compaction by raising it again! This physical lift and shift in the soil breaks the compacted areas allowing pore space to increase and effectively cracks the compact layers. To relieve compaction we can hollow tine (as this physically lifts pieces of soil, thatch and turf out of the lawn) or fork. With forking, once the tines have penetrated the surface do not simply pull it back out, but lean back on the fork until you see the soil lift. This forces the tines upward and lifts the soil profile. The fork can then be righted to the start position and lifted out carefully. This is a time consuming, but very beneficial process for soil maintenance.

How to aerate

Working in straight lines up and down or across the lawn, you should ensure that all areas are treated similarly and evenly. You should watch the spacing between the holes. The greater the number of holes the greater the benefits, although physically this will be more tiring to cover the lawned area. It is recommended that the spacing and depth of the aerating tines is varied every couple of years. Ideal spacing is somewhere between 4 – 6 inches on each penetration and the depth varied between 3 to 10 inches.

SCARIFICATION

Introduction

Scarification is a common and important maintenance practice used to combat the effects of thatch building up in a lawn. For the home-owner, it is commonly practiced as a manual maintenance operation using a multi-toothed rake. The rake is forcefully pulled over the entire surface of the lawn to remove leaf and thatch debris form the area. When carried out thoroughly, it is quite a severe maintenance procedure although the benefits gained afterward far outweigh the initial damaging effects.

What is thatch?

Thatch is the build up of organic matter under the canopy of the grass leaves but found on-top of the surface of the soil. It is defined as a tightly intermingled layer of living, dying and dead plant material, consisting of stolons, rhizomes, stems, crowns, nodes, and leaves. In fact, all parts of the turf grass plant.

FIG. 20 – THE AFTER EFFECTS OF SCARIFYING

FIG. 21 – THATCH, BELOW THE GRASS LEAVES, BUT ABOVE THE SOIL LAYER

FIG. 22 – HEAVY DUTY SCARIFYING BLADES

Although some thatch is good in a lawn, excessive amounts tend to act as a harbour for pests and diseases, give the lawn a spongy, very soft effect and hold applied nutrients within its cortex. This encourages increased root development in this area further exacerbating the problem. Heavily thatched lawns tend to exhibit poor drought tolerance and have an increased incidence of pest and disease attack.

A shallow layer of thatch – say around 5 – 10mm is actually good for your lawn because this not only acts as a barrier to prevent excessive loss of moisture from the soil but, also helps prevent wear on the surface and gives the lawn its familiar soft, cushioning effect.

When to scarify

During the late spring you can give the lawn a light scarification to remove any debris and leaf litter that has built up over the winter months. If your lawn suffers from heavy thatch problems then the ideal time to scarify will be the Autumn. If a heavy scarification is needed then it is advisable to fertilise one or two weeks before the operation is carried out to aid a rapid and full recovery. Wherever scarification is carried out be sure not to neglect irrigation afterward because this will also aid the recovery of the damaged sward.

How to scarify

BY HAND – Press the multi-toothed rake into the sward then vigorously pull vertically back towards you, keeping the downward pressure on the handle. The entire lawn should be covered and it is practical to carry this out in two directions (90°) where a thick thatch layer is experienced.

BY MACHINE – Some specialist garden centres will sell scarifying machinery and most hire shops will stock and hire them to the general public. It is advised that if you have severe thatch problems you hire or buy specialist kit for this purpose because raking the entire lawn to remove a thick thatch layer can be a tiring and time consuming operation.

Lightly raking the lawn

Frequent, very light raking of the lawn will give a number of benefits to the grasses - (a) it picks up the grass giving a cleaner cut when mowing; (b) it allows more light to enter into the grass canopy encouraging a thicker lawn; and, (c) it keeps the surface open, aiding the ingress of oxygen, fertilisers and water into the sward.

It is worthwhile investing in a good spring-tine rake because not only is it the ideal tool for the this, but also doubles as the ideal moss remover if moss control operations need to be carried out.

FIG. 23 – SISIS SCARIFYING UNIT

TOP DRESSING

· ·

Introduction

Top-dressing is the application of a soil or organic material to the surface of the lawn. It can be made up of a mixture of minerals such as sand, silt and clay, be an organic material such as peat or a mixture of all. Top dressing involves the application of texture and/or structure improving materials to the surface of the lawn and can be applied monthly, annually or bi-annually. It is the most effective method of improving minor surface irregularities in the lawn.

Top dressings are applied to lawns to help produce a smooth and level surface. Many lawns will eventually lose their smoothness and become uneven due to the stresses caused from children's play, turf repair work, disease attack, the removal of weeds or simply natural sink age. A frequent, light, top dressing rectifies this situation while also helping when mowing because the smooth surface will allow the mower to produce an even and consistent level of cut.

Ideally, any material applied to a lawn will be salt, stone and lime free. Sand based dressings can be incorporated into lawns by top dressing to improve soil aeration, water movement into and through the soil and help to reduce a soils tendency to compact. In contrast, finer textured materials, such as loam and organic matter are incorporated to enhance water and nutrient retention. Heavily organic top dressings are best avoided as these can encourage thatch build up and tend to encourage a shallow rooting grass plant and are a sure way to guarantee a surface that stays constantly wet!

If poor drainage has been a problem then top dressing with sand or sandy material can improve the ease at which water moves through a soil. The sandy material should be thoroughly worked into the lawn until it fills all the holes left from aerating work. In a similar way, if your lawn is prone to drought then finer top dressing materials can be added and worked in to improve water retention rates.

The benefits of top dressing

Top dressings are used on lawns to bring some or all of the following benefits:

1. Improve the levels of smoothness
2. Reduce and dilute the levels of thatch
3. Improve surface and soil drainage rates
4. Cover stony surfaces with new turf
5. Fill in cracks on newly laid turf
6. Increase water and nutrient retention
7. Allows the mower to produce a smooth and even cut

When to top dress

Top dressing the lawn can be carried out when necessary although historically, it has been carried out as part of the autumn renovation procedure. Top dressing will ideally be applied after any aerating procedures and scarification operations have been carried out because this allows the dressing to 'key' into the surface and soil below.

Weather and soil conditions should be dry and the forecast should be good (no heavy rain) for at least two or three days after the dressing has been applied. Ensure that your dressing material is also in a dry condition and is suitably placed for spreading over the entire lawn surface.

How to apply top dressings

Initially, the top dressing material should be broadcast lightly and evenly over the entire lawn using a shovel. You may decide to divide the lawn into strips using a garden line to aid you with application. The dressing should then be thoroughly worked into the base of the sward using the back of a rake, a lute or something similar. The idea is to push and pull the dressing along the surface removing it from the lumps and bumps and depositing it into the hollows. If carried out repeatedly over a period of one or two years the lawn will eventually become smooth and even.

Top dressings can be applied either lightly and frequently or heavily and infrequently. Light and frequent dressings ensure that thatch build-up is prevented, will keep the surface smooth throughout the year and require the least amount of physical exertion. Heavy, infrequent dressings are best applied to lawns that are in need of soil modification, such as a lawn that is in need of improving its drainage rates. Heavy dressings should be applied after aeration work has been carried out and you must ensure that any excess material is not left on the lawn because it will smother the grass, eventually killing it off.

WEED CONTROL AND MANAGEMENT

Introduction

The most common used definition for a weed is that of a plant growing out of place or a plant growing where it is not wanted. Within terms of the turf grass community its definition can be expanded to being an undesirable plant. In a lawn, weeds may be tolerated in small amounts but, eventually, due to their fierce competition for light, water and nutrients they must be either destroyed or removed. Lastly, weeds look unsightly and can distract the eye when admiring a well manicured and cared for lawn.

Weeds should not always be regarded as unsightly, or, perhaps, ugly plants, because there are many cottage gardens that are beautified and brought to life through the inclusion and encouragement of different species of weed plant. Of course, in this environment the term weed is not factually correct as the plant is no longer growing out of place!

Weeds, by nature, can be difficult to eradicate from lawned areas as many are extremely vigorous in growth, can withstand extremes in climate and can recover from wear just as effectively as the grass plant. Weeds spread mainly by seed and this seed can stay dormant in the soil for many years after the mother plant has died off. Annual weeds can also cause large bare areas when they die back after their growing period and lifespan has elapsed.

The most troublesome weeds are the perennial type that can survive and develop for a number of years and, if they have a prostrate (horizontal) growing nature, they can evade the blade of the lawn mower. In most cases, annual and biennial weeds can be controlled by regular mowing, although there are always some that can tolerate this maintenance operation.

A clean seed-bed is the ideal starting place to ensure a clean lawn (see page 14). From here, it is advised to kill off weeds as they appear rather than allowing huge populations to develop before adopting any type of control method. Boxing off grass clippings helps to prevent weeds spreading

FIG. 24 – WEED DYING AFTER SPAYING

in established lawns, but, the most effective weed deterrent, is that of keeping and maintaining a dense, thick, healthy lawn. If the grass plant population is dense and tightly knit then weeds stand little chance of establishing because there will not be enough light for them to utilise as well as no space for them grow.

Controlling weeds

The best way to control a weed is to firstly establish the species of weed present. Once we have established the type of weed, the correct herbicide can be used for control. Different species of weed will exhibit different life-spans - annuals live for one year only, but produce hundreds of seeds; biennials live for two growing seasons; whilst perennials can live longer with their roots persisting in the soil even though their aerial shoots die back during the winter. Some perennials spread by 'runners' over and through the ground sprouting new plants over a wide area, while others grow very deep into the soil via a 'tap root'. So when removing stubborn, seemingly 'concreted in' weeds by hand, it is wise to remember that even the smallest amount of root remaining can regenerate itself into a new plant.

Weeds are generally killed by using a hoe to cut and lift them from the ground. In lawns this is not an effective way to either remove or eradicate them. There are tools available to help in weed removal from lawns. An example being the 'daisy grubber' - a tool that is specifically made for removing weeds by hand. A simple household knife can also be used to good effect. However, are these tools always effective? - the answer is a resounding 'no'!

Most frequently, lawn weeds are treated with chemicals such as herbicides or to be more precise **'selective herbicides'**. These select the weeds from the grass plants and eventually see to their death leaving the grass healthy and in-tact. This can be done safely if you are clear on which selective herbicide to use and when to use it. Not all weed killers are deadly poisonous! Nevertheless, all should be applied with care, with the correct equipment for application, the correct personal attire and with the environment at large in mind.

To CONTROL ANNUAL WEEDS – Ideally, these will be killed before they have a chance to seed. Where possible, kill these while they are still germinating, young plants. By cultivating a bare soil quite regularly you can encourage the soils 'stock' of seeds to germinate, thereby eliminating the seed bank stored within it. Annual seeds have a habit of appearing and surviving in composted materials. To prevent this, ensure you do not allow weeds to grow on top of your compost heap and ensure it is fully composted before using it.

To CONTROL PERENNIAL WEEDS – Perennial weeds grow for two or more growing seasons, they are able to survive drought and wear, have the ability to regenerate tand enter a state of dormancy when weather conditions are cold and not conducive to growth. Their root systems have the ability to spread extensively and deeply through a soil and these roots have the ability to reproduce a new plant from the smallest portion left in the soil. It is recommended that perennial weeds are killed during their seedling stage before the tap root has begun to develop fully. Treatment with the correct herbicide may need repeated applications before death occurs.

The advantages of using herbicides

When using a herbicide there is no need to disturb the soil in any way. The target plant will be killed off with the minimum of fuss and effort leaving minimal surface disruption. Herbicides can effectively kill off colonised weeds, including their roots and stems and therefore prevent re-infestation. They can control weeds

of all sizes and give a quick response once applied.

Timing of application

There are two main categories of selective weed killer, systemic and contact. Systemic herbicides can be applied at any time during the year when the plant is growing actively. The ideal time for application of herbicides will be late April/early May or during Autumn when generally, excellent results will be achieved. Systemic chemicals are absorbed into the leaves and stems and then spread through the plants vascular system to kill it off rapidly. You will find that most lawn weed killers purchased in garden centres have this form of action. If the herbicide is applied during Spring or Autumn, the surrounding grasses will also be at their most active and will quickly and efficiently fill in the gaps left.

Contact herbicides will kill only the green parts of the plant with which they come into contact. Contact herbicides are most effective against annual type weeds because with the perennial type they do not affect the root system allowing them to regenerate once the green aerial leaves have died. Contact herbicides are best used as a defence during the colder, more dormant period of the year where growth is at its minimum.

Total weed killers

Total weed killers kill everything with which they come into contact. Generally, the active ingredient used is glyphosate which will wipe out weeds, sedges, and grass, in fact anything green! Only use a total weed killer on pavements or other hard standing areas and keep well away from grassed areas or your lawn unless you wish to kill off everything and start again!

How to apply weed killers

Try to leave the grass and, therefore, weeds uncut for at least three days before application of the herbicide. This allows for a greater leaf area and therefore target area for the herbicide to come into contact with. Once applied, do not mow for a period of at least three days to allow the herbicide time to move effectively through the weed and ultimately kill it. It is also advisable not to collect clippings for composting for at least one month after spraying. On newly seeded lawns wait until the germinating plants have had

at least two months to establish before applying any herbicide because a young grass sward can be damaged. Always read and follow the manufacturers' recommendations for use and avoid exposing your skin to the chemical mixtures.

A little advice

Before resorting to herbicides, try managing weeds by improving the general condition of the lawn and doing some occasional hand weeding. If you decide that a pesticide is necessary, follow these steps:

1. Before buying, make sure that the pesticide label has directions for use on lawns and lists the pest you want to control. Apply the product only where the pest

is found; spot treat instead of applying broadly

2. Always read and follow the instructions on the label. The label will give you the directions for use, including how much to apply and when. It will also indicate whether protective clothing, gloves or equipment are needed

3. Store pesticides out of the reach of children and pets and buy only the amount you expect to use in one season or for that occasion.

4. Make sure you do not apply a weed-killer containing Glyphosate to grass areas unless you want to kill grass completely.

WEED IDENTIFICATION The following pictures and text will aid you in the correct identification of the most common weed types found in lawns.

YARROW – *Achillea millefolium*

Yarrow increases both vegetatively and by seed so mowing may prevent it from seeding however, the weed will still spread horizontally by slender underground stems. These grow slowly then turn upward to produce new plants. There are many weed killers that yarrow is not susceptible to, so those chosen must contain 2,4-D, MCPA with dicamba or Mecoprop-P. This treatment may need to be repeated. During dry conditions the plant can be pulled out of the lawn by hand and this may extract the underground stems as well.

FIELD WOODRUSH – *Luzula campestris*

Found in many lawns that have a slightly acidic or acidic nature and in lawns that have low levels of nutrients within them. Field woodrush will produce both flowers (seed) and spread itself vegetatively via short creeping stems. It is very resistant to most selective herbicides and is therefore very difficult to eradicate by these means. The best control is through hand weeding the individual plants from the lawn. Field woodrush takes on a similar appearance to grass but its leaves are both broader and thicker and are covered by long white hairs. Chemically, some control may be gained by repeated (two or three) applications of Mecoprop-P or 2,4-D with Mecoprop-P.

LESSER TREFOIL – *Trifolium dubium*

Lesser trefoil is an annual weed commonly found in lawns. It is able to survive even the closest mowing and can grow to become abundant in a lawn. It especially likes impoverished, poorly maintained lawns. Flowering from May to October it produces many seeds that germinate in the Spring and Autumn. This weed has very small, grass coloured, leaves that creep horizontally through the lawn making it difficult to identify and spot as it infests an area. It is best to control this weed before it seeds because it is very resistant to selective herbicides. However, as the leaves and stems creep outwards, they can be gently pulled upward until the mother plant is found and removed by hand. If you do treat using chemicals, repeated treatments will be required before effective control is gained. Use products containing a number of active ingredients if you are to control using herbicides.

YORKSHIRE FOG – *Holcus lanatus*

This weed is actually a grass, so it cannot be killed off with the application of a 'selective herbicide'. This grass species is regarded as a weed because of its broad large leaf area. It also exhibits a poor yellow/green leaf colour. Yorkshire fog is commonly found in lawns across the UK and is well adapted to growing in most soil conditions. It forms dense patches of grass throughout the lawn. Yorkshire fog is also commonly found in golf greens as it can tolerate an extremely low cutting height. Best identified by looking at the base of the plant, here you should see hairy stems with pink striations running upward from the base on the plant on each individual stem. Yorkshire Fog can be controlled by slashing the plant with a sharp knife (a Stanley Knife is ideal) consistently for a number of weeks or by digging the affected area out of the lawn.

DAISY – *Bellis perennis*

FIG. COURTESY OF LAURENCE GALE MSc – www.pitchcare.com

Perhaps the most common lawn weed to be found, daisy can grow on all types of soils. A perennial weed that propagates itself both by seed and vegetatively, although vegetative spread is very slow. Daisy is very effective at flowering and seeding in even the lowest cut of lawns. It is relatively easy to remove the plant by hand weeding, but the most effective control will be gained by application of herbicides if the weed infests large portions of the lawn. The active ingredients; 2,4-D, MCPA with dicamba or Mecoprop-P will all control this weed, although repeated application may be required for total eradication.

SHEEP'S SORREL – *Rumex acetosella*

FIG. COURTESY OF RANDELL G. PROSTAK – UNIVERSITY OF MASSACHUSETTS

Common on acid soil situations, this weed can also grow in neutral pH soils. Spreading quickly by its creeping habit it is one of the few weeds that can produce new shoots from any part of its extensive root system. Flowering from May to August, it sometimes produces seeds although this is unlikely in regularly mown lawns. Most selective weed killers will give control but, due to the extensive root system, repeated application will be needed to control this weed effectively. Weed killers containing the active ingredient Mecoprop-P should not be used because Sheep's sorrel is resistant to it.

LESSER CELANDINE – *Ranunculus ficaria*

Found in many lawns, this lawn can sometimes be mistaken for daisy. This weed can grow almost anywhere. The differences between this and the daisy are that lesser celandine has heart shaped leaves and pure yellow flowers. There are two forms of this weed - one that produces seeds and another that produces bulbils in the axils of the leaves. It is the bulbil type that is the most common in gardens. The bulbils are small plants with a bud and a root which establish themselves as a new plant when shed by the mother plant. In lawns, lesser celandine is a troublesome weed to eradicate because of its resistance to weed killers. However, repeated treatments with a selective herbicide containing mostly MCPA will give some control. If only small areas of the lawn are infested it, is best to kill the weak and surrounding grass with a total weed killer such as glyphosate and then re-turf later.

GREATER PLANTAIN – *Plantago major*

Greater plantain is the most commonly found species of plantain and loves to grow in weak, sparse and thin growing lawns. The leaves lie very flat on the ground enabling it to avoid the mower blades. Flowering from May to September, it produces masses of seeds that are used to re-infect the lawn in later years. The active ingredients 2,4-D, MCPA with dicamba or Mecoprop-P will all control this weed easily.

WHITE CLOVER - *Trifolium repens*

This type of clover will commonly be found in lawns. It forms rather obvious patches that can be seen to flower even on regularly mown surfaces. As this weed can grow in between and around the grass leaves, it proves to be almost impossible to remove by hand weeding. The seeds it produces are capable of lasting up to 20 years in the soil. White clover also propagates itself vegetatively using creeping stems that root as they spread. Control of this weed is never easy and, although most lawn weed killers will have some effect, white clover is very resistant to them. For best control only use the active ingredients ioxynil and/or Mecoprop-P and these will need repeated treatments for a number of years before good results are seen.

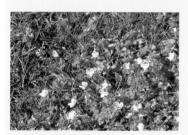

SLENDER SPEEDWELL - *Veronica filiformis*

Unusually, this weed does not form seeds but only spreads itself vegetatively by creeping stems. It is capable of rapidly spreading through a lawn and once established is difficult to remove because it can reproduce from cut off pieces of stem. Slender speedwell is relatively difficult to control in lawns, but weed killers containing Mecoprop-P can effectively kill it if repeated applications are made.

CAT'S EAR - *Hypochaeris radicata*

A perennial weed that looks very similar to the dandelion except that the leaves are a lot thicker and have small white hairs growing out of them. This weed will be seen in the lawn throughout the year and can easily be removed by hand weeding. The active ingredients; 2,4-D, MCPA with dicamba or Mecoprop-P will all control this weed if repeated applications are laid on the lawn.

DANDELION – *Taraxacum officinale*

FIG. COURTESY OF LAURENCE GALE MSc – www.pitchcare.com

Dandelions will grow in just about any soil or under any environmental conditions. They can flower for the majority of the year, May to October but mostly do so during the Spring. If the dandelion is allowed to produce seed heads – due to infrequent mowing – the ultra light weight seeds are easily dispersed by the wind to other parts of the lawn. The weed is best controlled chemically because it produces a very deep tap root that can reproduce a new plant if the smallest part is left in the soil. If you plan to hand weed dandelion, then it is suggested that the entire plant is dug around and out to ensure none of the root survives. Repeated applications with any of the active ingredients 2,4-D, MCPA with dicamba or Mecoprop-P will control this weed.

RIBWORT PLANTAIN – *Plantago lanceolata*

Ribwort is a common perennial weed both of lawns and arable grassland, it is widespread throughout the UK and can be found growing on a wide range of soils. Ribwort plantain is quite a variable species so the picture exhibited here may not represent wholly the type you have growing in your lawn. This weed survives well in lawns even where the lawn is mown at a short height of cut.

Flowering begins in April and continues throughout the year but this weed may not flower at all in closely mown swards. Control is best managed by hand picking out the germinating plants early in the Spring. Applications of MCPA, Mecoprop-P and Dicamba will also control this weed adequately.

CREEPING BUTTERCUP – *Ranunculus repens*

This weed is common in gardens throughout the UK and is very proficient at colonising once established. Creeping buttercup can be found on a large variety of soils ranging from damp to dry. Creeping buttercup will flower - with bright yellow petals – anytime from May until August during the year. Due to its creeping growing habit this weed may well encroach onto the lawn from a flower bed or the lawns. Control is best managed with hand weeding though applications of fluroxpyr, clopralid and MCPA

Weeds of newly sown grass

Many weeds encountered on freshly sown turf are not lawn weeds but weeds of arable soils,. These tend to die out quickly once mowing operations commence. You may wish to choose to ignore the growth of these and simply leave them until the growing conditions allow mowing to begin. Typically, the following weeds may be found:

Shepherd's purse (*Capsella bursa-pastoris*)

Fat Hen (*Chenopodium album*)

Dead Nettle (*Lamium purpureum*)

Groundsel (*Senecio vulgaris*)

Spurrey (*Spergula arvensis*)

Chickweed (*Stellaria media*)

DISEASE CONTROL AND MANAGEMENT

Introduction

Diseases will commonly affect turf lawns. It is said that the key to avoiding disease attack is to apply good husbandry to the lawn.

The key to the management of diseases is to be aware of the environments they prefer and the grass species they attack. To a great extent we can influence the environment that determines or deters disease growth with the management styles and practices we carry out or implement. So, the over-application of fertiliser, over-application of water, using materials for top dressing high in lime or calcium that will significantly alter the surface pH, or by creating shade or environments where the air movement over the lawn is minimal (usually from the planting or fences we erect around the lawn or garden) may all lead to problems. Also, closely linked with disease development is the amount of thatch your lawn holds because many diseases or fungi survive and over-winter in this layer waiting for

FIG. 25 – FUSARIUM PATCH (COURTESY OF PAM SHERRATT, OHIO STATE UNIVERSITY)

the ideal environmental conditions before attacking the grass plant.

This section is devoted to the diseases most frequently associated with lawns. If you do suffer from an attack of lawn disease you can use the following pages initially to identify the specific type of disease you have and then use the correct chemical fungicide to control and limit its severity. Also listed are the cultural control methods that you can implement to prevent further or future attacks of the disease.

Fusarium patch

Fusarium patch is a turf disease caused by the fungus Microdochium nivale. The disease was first recorded in the thirties and at the time was quoted as being, "the commonest, most disfiguring and damaging disease of turf known".

The disease develops as small dead patches of grass. Upon closer examination the dead area may be water-soaked and fused together and there may be an orange/brown or off- white coloured ring of fluffy material (mycelium) around the outer edge. These dead patches tend to join together to form larger areas of scarring. During less severe attacks the turf grass surface may just exhibit small bleached/brown dead circular scars.

Generally, the disease can be easily controlled with the application of a correct fungicide (see table below)

Cultural control methods to prevent attack in the first place include thatch reduction and techniques such as scarification also should be carried out and any excess surface moisture should be reduced by ensuring the lawn drains correctly and efficiently. Avoid early Spring or late Autumn fertiliser applications, especially those containing nitrogen (N). Check and improve if necessary the amount of light the lawn receives and trim

FIG. 26 – FUSARIUM PATCH

back or remove material that may be causing shade. The pH level of top dressings put on the turf surface should not be too alkaline because this may encourage the development of the disease.

Take-all patch

Take-all patch is caused by the fungus Gaeumannomyces graminis and was formally known as Ophiobolus graminis or Ophiobolus patch. It was first discovered on a lawn in Amersfoort in Holland in 1931.

The disease will mainly affect the bent grass species but can also attack other grasses albeit. Less severely. In the primary stages of the disease it is most noticeable during the late Summer and Autumn, especially when the weather has been particularly droughty. The first signs are that of the infected plants becoming bleached or bronzed in colour and forming dead circular areas across the lawn. These may become depressed as the thatch layer is consumed by the fungus. The dead grass will be very easy to pull up as this disease rots the base of the plant. Another trait of take-all patch is that weeds and other grasses (not Agrostis species) can grow and survive an attack and these can be seen in the centre of the dead saucer shaped area.

Cultural control methods for this disease involve ensuring the surface stays in a dry condition, ensuring the lawn does not develop excessive thatch, ensuring that any

FIG. 27 – COURTESY OF DR. KARL DANNEBERGER, OHIO STATE UNIVERSITY

fertiliser/s applied are done so at the correct time of year and that heavy and frequent applications of water are avoided. Sudden changes that raise the surface pH (make it more alkaline) or lawns grown on alkaline soils may make the grasses more susceptible to this disease and aid the development of the fungus, so care should be taken that any dressings applied to the lawn are not too high in pH (above 6.5).

FIG. 28 – COURTESY OF LAURENCE GALE MSc., www.pitchcare.com

Red thread

Red thread is caused by the fungus laetisaria fuciformis and was previously known as Corticium disease or Corticium fuciformis.

The effect on the grass plant is initially exhibited by withered and brown leaf tips then eventually the whole grass plant or leaf will turn brown. If you look closely at the affected plants you may see small red coloured threads or needles protruding from the leaf blades (hence the name red thread) and spotting these is a sure and very convenient method of diagnosis. In severe cases the entire affected area will be seen as having a red tinge. The patches affected do not form circles or shapes and there is no distinct pattern to the diseased grasses although affected areas eventually join together to form mottled areas of dead plants. The most susceptible grasses for this disease are the fescues (Festuca species) and ryegrasses (Lolium species).

FIG. 29 – COURTESY OF PAM SHERRATT, OHIO STATE UNIVERSITY

CONTROL – Red thread particularly enjoys damp, shaded conditions but has also been frequently identified during the drier summer months. It is associated with under-nourished lawns (especially those lacking in nitrogen) and prefers acid to neutral pH levels.

Cultural control methods for this are simple, good, lawn husbandry which, together with ensuring that the lawn is adequately fertilised, free draining and actively growing, should prevent attack. If the disease does attack, the best method to curtail it is to apply a nitrogenous fertiliser. Although if the attack is particularly severe chemical application maybe necessary. In severe cases the lawn clippings should be collected and disposed of to curtail spread and development.

FIG. 30 – COURTESY OF PAM SHERRATT, OHIO STATE UNIVERSITY

Fairy ring

The term 'fairy ring' has its origin from myth and superstition which believed a fairy ring to be the result of a circle of dancing pixies (fairies). Others thought them to be the result of lightning strikes and also – strangely enough - the area where the devil churned his butter!

Today we know that fairy rings are the result of a number of different species of fungi colonising the soil, leaf litter or thatch. The breakdown of organic matter in and on the soil caused by this fungal activity releases nitrogen which stimulates grass on the outside of the ring causing it to grow taller and darker than the surrounding grasses.

The band (ring) of stimulated grass can sometimes be associated with the fruiting bodies (mushrooms, toadstools and puffballs) of the fungus. Some of these can be poisonous and are best picked and disposed if young children frequently play on the lawn. Removing these fruiting bodies will

FIG. 31 - TYPE 1 FAIRY RING (COURTESY OF PAM SHERRATT, OHIO STATE UNIVERSITY)

not weaken the fungus, although it will improve that aesthetics of the area.

There are three different types of fairy ring:

TYPE 1 – Those that kill the grass off or badly damage it

TYPE 2 – Those that stimulate grass growth only

TYPE 3 - Those that cause no damage to the turf but fruiting bodies can be seen

CONTROL – Fairy ring type 1 and 2 are invariably difficult to control, both chemically and culturally. Application of chemicals is not always effective because fungicides typically kill all fungi, including those which compete with the fairy ring fungi. Control of fairy ring from fungicides has, therefore, traditionally been a hit or miss affair. Type three is best managed by simple collection of the mushrooms, etc, as they appear.

Fairy ring is heavily associated with a lawns organic matter content, so control of this – namely the thatch content – can prevent or limit the severity of an attack, as can regular aeration work. Digging fairy ring out of the lawn is one method used to remove fairy ring from the lawn, but this is considered a hit and miss affair because simply dropping a small amount of the fungus in the soil from the shovel or spade onto unaffected areas can cause a new attack.

Applications of nitrogen or iron can help mask the lush green, high growth areas around the

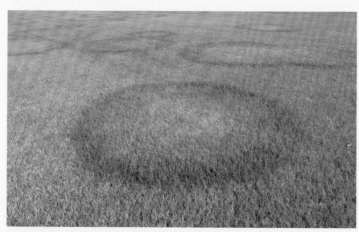

FIG. 32 - TYPE 2 FAIRY RING (COURTESY OF DR. DAVID GARDNER, OHIO STATE UNIVERSITY)

ring that make it stand out in the lawn and some success has been gained by soaking the soil around the ring area for a number of weeks. However, this soaking method should be avoided where fairy rings are numerous across the lawn because it may simply aid the spread of the disease.

FIG. 33 - TYPICAL SYMPTOMS OF FAIRY RING TYPE 3 (COURTESY OF LAURENCE GALE MSc., WWW.PITCHCARE.COM)

Anthracnose

This disease is generally found to affect lawns that have low nutrient levels and compacted soils. The corrective actions are straightforward.

Anthracnose can appear in a couple of forms and, as such, can generally be found attacking the grass plant during anytime of the year. As with red thread, the symptoms of this disease do not take on any particular form but, the diseased areas will join together and form larger areas of dead plant tissue and scarring.

FIG. 34 - COURTESY OF DR. KARL DANNEBERGER, OHIO STATE UNIVERSITY

When under attack the grass plant will initially turn yellow and the youngest leaves may also appear to have a red tinge to them. Eventually, the area will turn brown as the plants die back. This disease particularly likes to attack the grass species Poa annua (Annual Meadow Grass – See grasses guide) and, if this species of grass is prevalent in the sward and the conditions mentioned above are also present, the likelihood of anthracnose attack is high.

Cultural control methods to combat the effects of this disease include ensuring that you have satisfactory levels of nutrients in the soil for plant uptake and that any compaction in the soil is treated correctly. Anthracnose will also quickly spread itself under wet soil conditions, so ensure the surface of the lawn is as free draining as possible.

LAWN PESTS

Introduction

There are many different kinds of pests that live in grass and lawns. Some are visible to the naked eye while others are too small to be seen. The majority of turf grass pests do little damage to the plant and can be tolerated in the lawn but, occasionally, pests can become troublesome, cause extensive injury to the grass plant and become a major problem. Luckily ,with the climate we have here in northern Europe, insect damage is usually limited to sporadic, occasional problems

Some of the damage symptoms that insects and pests can cause to the lawn are very similar to those caused by diseases so it is very important to correctly diagnose the problem before treatment is applied. The best and simplest method to determine the underlying cause is careful observation. In most cases where the lawn has been damaged enough to be noticeable, the organism can be easily seen on or near the surface. The following section of the book looks

FIG. 35 - LEATHERJACKET LARVAE ON TURF SURFACE (COURTESY OF CHRIS MITCHELL)

closely at the problems, symptoms and causes of pest attack.

The Grubs

The grubs of some insect species survive just under the surface of the leaves and feed on the roots, stems and crowns of the grass plant. In the worst cases, the grass attacked by these grubs can be extensive causing the death of large areas of turf .

Leatherjackets

These are the grubs of the common crane-fly (Tipulidea species) or 'daddy long-legs'. They are perhaps the most common lawn turf pest.

SYMPTOMS – The grey/brown larvae grow up to 5 cm long, live in the soil just below the surface and feed on turf grass roots, stems and sometimes leaves. Most damage occurs on the youngest plants in the Spring, although they may also develop in the late autumn. The effected grass plants initially turn yellow, wilt and then die. High populations in lawns cause yellow patches during dry weather and affected areas may also develop further damage from birds probing and tearing at the soil to extract the leatherjackets

BIOLOGY – Adult crane flies emerge from the pupae in the soil during August or September and, after mating, the female is capable of laying over 300 eggs in the soil. The eggs hatch a fortnight later and the larvae feed on the roots during the Autumn and again the following Spring.

Chafer grubs

The larvae of at least five different species of chafer beetle (Scarabaeidae sp.), also known as white grub, can live in the soil of lawns. Both larvae and adults can attack the grass plant.

SYMPTOMS – C-shaped, soft white larvae, up to 40mm long with a brown head and six legs (on the upper part of the body) feed on the roots, stems and sometimes leaves of the grass plant. The grass may appear yellow or brown before wilting and dying. During dry weather ,brown withered turf can be seen and the chafer grub can be found if the turf is lifted. The symptoms are similar to those found with leatherjackets.

BIOLOGY – The biology of all five main chafers found in lawns and gardens is similar. The females will lay their eggs in the soil near the grass plant during the Summer and the larvae hatch a few weeks later. The grubs will then mainly feed on the grass roots until they are ready to pupate and emerge the following Spring.

Frit fly

Not a common pest of turf grasses but it can become an occasional problem. The frit fly (Oscinella frit) larvae are 3-4 mm long, yellow/brown in colour with black, curved mouth hooks.

SYMPTOMS – The larvae are stem-boring grubs that can stunt the growth of the grass plant. Under severe attacks the plant will die. Where the lawn is regularly mown, attack will be limited because the larvae prefer grass plants that are fully developed.

BIOLOGY – The larvae over-winter on grasses and pupate in the spring. The small (2-3mm long) adults emerge during May/June and the females lay their eggs near the bases of grass plants. The eggs will hatch one week later, then the larvae will enter young shoots to feed for a period of two or three weeks.. The larvae pupate in late June or early July within damaged plants or from the soil. A second generation of adults emerge July or August and then a third generation emerge during the Autumn. On each occasion eggs will be laid.

Control of grub problems

Many of the insecticides used to control grub problems have now been banned from use because they were deemed too polluting and dangerous to the environment. As a consequence, there is very little one can do to control attack from insect grubs.

It is advised that you contact your local garden centre for advice on what is currently on the market and available to control such problems.

Another good source of information, as well as for purchasing goods suitable for control, is the internet, although many of the products claiming to control problems may not be proven and/or reliable. The last solution will be to hire a professional garden service to advise you on the current legislation and practice concerning chemical application.

Other pests

Ants

Can cause damage to the plant from disturbing the soil around and underneath it sometimes causing root and eventual plant death. If the colony is big enough, this soil disturbance can take the form of small soil heaps which can be seen around the lawn. Ants occasionally dismantle and damage the grass plant leaves.

If ants are a particular problem on your lawn there is really little you can do. Don't be tempted to put down powdered ant killer (usually a white powder) as this is not effective and leaves your lawn looking terrible. One effective method used – though it will take 2–3 months to see results – is to lay down 'Nippon' gels traps near the nest's entrance/exit points. The colony will take this sugary, but deadly gel down to feed others. With persistance, you should see noticable results. Note: caution is required using this method where young children and pets are present in the garden.

Worms

Worms are not necessarily a pest of lawns as they do more good than harm. However, the bad takes the form of perhaps hundreds or thousands of unsightly castings over the surface of the lawn. These castings can smother the grass around them when mowing, stick to the mowers roller, creating mud and mess around the lawn, create a slippery surface, stick to your shoes, look unsightly and, when flattened, actually make the ideal bed for weed seeds to develop upon. Lastly, high earthworm populations will encourage moles!

It should be noted that earthworms are found in all healthy soils, although they have a preference for organic, heavy soils of neutral to alkaline pH. They are constantly feeding on the organic matter within the soil, in fact, the thatch layer is one of their favourite places to be and to this end they provide control for you free of charge! Their burrows and runs allow gases to exchange between the soil and the atmosphere, provide drainage channels to help water into and through the soil, while also helping the soil warm up quickly in the spring.

Earthworm activity is at its most active during the Spring and Autumn (generally more so during the Autumn) with less activity seen during the dryer, droughtier Summer months when they tend to bury deeper into the soil and therefore stop casting.

Control of earthworm populations is not an easy task! The chemicals once used to destroy them have now been banned and there currently are no specific, effective chemical controls on the market. Adopting the correct cultural measures will help and much can be achieved by reducing the amount of thatch in the lawn and regular slitting and aeration

FIG. 36 – TYPICAL WORM CAST

FIG. 37 – MOLE HILLS

work that will dry out the surface faster discouraging them from the upper soil layers. Removing the grass clippings (another source of organic matter for food) and the restriction of applying organic top-dressings will all also help to discourage worm activity. Application of the fungicide carbendazim has been known to irritate worms and reduce their activity in grassed areas.

Moles

Moles are small, subterranean animals covered in a dark velvety fur that rummage around the garden area actively seeking out worms or small grubs to eat. Even though moles do not directly eat grass roots the damage they cause can be severe and it may take many months before the lawn full recovers after they have been removed or eradicated.

Typically, there will be large soil disturbances around the lawn area where the mole has pushed the excess soil up from its underground burrows and runs. The mounds will be joined underneath the surface by a network of tunnels. If the mole has tunnelled close enough to the surface sometimes the grass above may die or you will find that the surface collapses leading to undulating and uneven lawn surfaces.

Control can be gained by trapping or gassing with products such as

Luxan, Talunex or Phostoxin (both contain Aluminium phosphide). This is a simple operation, carried out by sealing all the surrounding mole hills (general compaction of the soil on the hill) then by dropping a tablet of Aluminium phosphide into the run. Once the tablet/s come into contact with the damp soil a gas is released which spreads throughout the network of tunnels. Trapping can be a rather cruel, long-winded affair unless it is carried out by someone with experience so it is advised that you employ a professional for this operation. Gassing and trapping of moles proves to be most effective from October through April when the moles are active, but before they have entered their breeding season.

Some fungicides containing carbendazim or thiophanate-methyl can be used to control earthworms and therefore deprive the moles of their food source. However, it is important to remember that earthworms are important components of soil aeration and general soil health.

Birds

Birds can cause damage to lawns when looking for a juicy grub or worm to eat. Rooks and other large birds will occasionally rip up turf and soil as they search and if your lawn suffers from this problem then it is likely you have a worm or grub problem of some kind (see above).

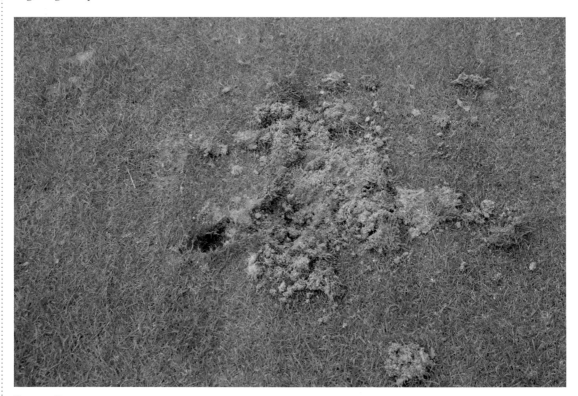

FIG. 38 – BIRD DAMAGE TO TURF AFTER SEARCHING FOR GRUBS

FIG. 39 – THE AFFECTS OF DOG URINE ON GRASS

It should be noted that on well established lawns birds eating grubs can be an effective control of a likely future problem.

When you have a newly sown lawn birds such as pigeons and starlings may become a problem by eating the seed you have sown. The best defence against this will be to erect a scarecrow of some kind or perhaps more effectively cover the area with a membranous germination sheet.

Dogs

Bitches (more so than dogs) can cause significant lawn damage throughout the year. Bitches produce fairly large amounts of urine in a concentrated spot and this can become toxic to the grass plant and kill it. Death of grass from urine typically will reveal itself as brown, dead, circular scars around the lawn that have a perimeter of lush growth around the dead area (caused by the nitrogen in the urine). Dogs tend to spend their time urinating over numerous bushes, fence posts or other plants marking out their territory. This is obviously less damaging to the grass as the urine can be away from the lawn or less concentrated if on the lawn.

NOTE - To prevent leaf yellowing or grass death from dog urine apply water to area immediately after. If you can be bothered of course!

The other problem dogs provide for lawns is their faeces and even though these do not necessarily kill the grass (unless they are particularly large and smother it!) they are a problem from a hygienic point of view, especially where children are present. Lawns covered in dog faeces (in varying states of decomposition) tend to encourage blue bottles and other large flies to the garden, these can then eventually make their way into your house.

MOSS CONTROL AND ERADICATION

Introduction

Typically, moss will encroach on most lawns at some point during their life. Moss in turf looks unsightly and makes the mowing operation difficult to carry out. Moss can have an affinity for water and many moss infected lawns can actually be hazardous places to be when walking over them, especially if the lawn slopes. During certain times of the year moss may well out-compete grass and actively colonise when the ideal environment conditions for growth are presented to it.

On lawns, mosses will grow rapidly when the following conditions are prevailing:

- Poorly draining, wet soils
- Where the soil is inadequately fertilised or lacking in nutrient content
- Areas where the air quality is poor
- On lawns with high levels of thatch within them

FIG. 40 – THE MOSS PLANT

- On compacted, hard soils
- Where shade is prevalent
- Where the grass is mown too closely leading to sparse and weak grass coverage
- On very dry or droughty soils

Moss can be easily controlled with chemicals, but unless the underlying conditions for its growth are either removed, improved or put right it is sure to re-colonise in the future.

Taking into account the bullet points above, you should examine the lawn and the surrounding area and rectify the problem/s leading to moss growth and development.

Before any control measures are taken you should take time to read the next paragraph and understand how moss develops and spreads and understand when the best time is to control it.

Types and development of moss

Moss reproduces itself via miniscule spores. These spores are produced by the plant twice in each growing season, once in the Spring and again during the Autumn. It is after producing the Autumn spores that the plant grows slowly through the Winter period before producing a final set of Spring spores after which the mother plant dies leaving the hundreds of thousands of spores to replace it. The mother plant will eventually die under the stresses of the first spell of hot weather as the summer period nears.

The spores are produced in a special capsule at the head of the moss plant and the plant itself actually dies from the bottom upward leaving the spore producing head to die last. It is therefore, imperative that you check that the entire plant is dead before trying to physically remove it from the lawn. If you neglect to do this and try to remove the plant with raking before death, you will only spread the spores over the lawn. It

is these spores that make the moss plant difficult to control because many of the operations we carry out in lawn maintenance will actually aid the spread of the spores.

Control of moss

If moss is present, it is initially best controlled using either calcinated sulphate of iron (the rate of application will be dependant upon what the manufacturer recommends) or lawn sand containing iron sulphate some may also contain ammonium sulphate. Ammonium sulphate gives the lawn a small spurt of growth to promote a speedy recovery of the grass and encourage the filling of the bare areas the moss leaves behind. Lawn sand can be applied at a rate of 100-125g per metre square and should be lightly irrigated after application.

When the treatment has been seen to be successful (usually around three weeks after application) the moss can be removed from the grass sward. Moss is removed from a lawn

in a number of ways such as using a fine-toothed sprung rake (Springbok rake), using a general garden rake or by mechanical scarifying the area. The dead moss should be removed from the lawn and not left to rot back to ensure that the grass surrounding and intertwined with it can recover as fast as possible and fill the voids left behind

Lichens

In Britain the most common leafy lichens are usually found in neglected lawns, in areas of low fertility, on moist, or seasonally dry and thatched turf. The body of a lichen consists of overlapping leafy structures with a white underneath and green/brown/blue upper leaf.

Control of lichens can be achieved by scarification followed by good cultural practices (See IPM pages 91-92). Any maintenance operation that increases grass vigour, such as aeration or fertilisation will help prevent re-invasion.

ORGANIC LAWN CARE

Why go organic?

If you find the idea of applying synthetic chemicals of any kind to your lawn unattractive, unsafe or environmentally unfriendly, then organic lawn care may be the alternative you should consider. It involves the implementation of a number of preset conditions designed to eradicate chemical inputs without sacrificing or compromising turf quality.

It has been postulated that many of the chemicals used as active ingredients in today's herbicides, fungicides' pesticides and fertilisers are linked to a number of problematic areas such as soil and groundwater pollution, toxicity to animals and possibly to humans.

The basic principles

The basic principles behind organic lawn husbandry involve carrying out a number of cultural maintenance practices that encourage strong grass growth and help to improve the levels of beneficial soil fungi and bacteria. Not only can raised populations of micro-flora be beneficial to grass growth but, also, are thought to help fight the effects of pests and diseases.

The following sub-headings list some organic methods of lawn care maintenance operations,. However, it should not be lost from sight that, if the cultural practices that are discussed throughout this book are implemented, you will be a long way down the road of best management practice and the requirements of chemical input should be minimal.

Basic lawn management techniques

As detailed in this book, ensure that you control the levels of thatch that appear within the lawn. Aerate and water the lawn only when necessary and mow frequently at a suitable height of cut

Mowing

Correct mowing techniques and heights will benefit your lawn in a number of ways. The higher the height of cut, then the greater the depth of root. The greater the depth of root, the more resistant the lawn will be to drought and disease stresses. Also, the plant will better utilise the nutrients available in the soil.

Mowing heights of 2.5" plus are generally recommended for organically maintained lawns. This increased mowing height helps the plant develop, fight disease and increases the leaf area available to sunlight, hence improved growth.

Carry out mowing operations on a regular basis, not only will this thicken the sward, but it will prevent the lawn being smothered with too many clippings that can prevent the grass from photosynthesising and growing between cuts. If the lawn clippings do smother the grasses beneath then hand rake the majority off. Of course, this will keep you in good condition too!

Keep the blades of your mower sharp and clean. Keeping the mower in good condition ensures it cuts cleanly and evenly every time and does not rip or tear at the grass blades. Ripped or torn leaf blades will weaken the grasses defences and may encourage disease entry into the plant. Try to

Using weed killers & pesticides

Try to remove weeds by picking them out by hand. Purchase a 'Daisy Grubber' from the garden centre (or use a dining knife – just as effective) and use this to extract the weed from the lawn. If weeding by hand is carried out monthly you will find the populations of weeds in the lawn will drastically reduce. Try to remove as much of the roots as possible, while at the same time try not to remove any grass plants or leave large bare patches where you have been.

The best defence against weeds is to manage your lawn correctly (as outlined in this book), over sow seed regularly and top dress regularly. A thick, dense lawn is the best defence because it blocks out the available sunlight, which will help prevent weed seeds from germinating.

It is thought that the over-use of herbicides such as 2, 4-D in home lawns has contributed to the increase in health problems to both children and pets. Studies have revealed problems developing when herbicides were applied to a home lawn more than four times per year.

Plant health

The best method to ensuring your lawn stays vigorous in growth and health is to ensure you choose and sow the correct grass species for your situation. Choose grasses that grow well and suit your particular environment and soil conditions. Do this and the lawn will prosper throughout the year. See tables 1–3 for further reading.

have the mower blades sharpened after every 8 hours use.

Fertilising

Fertilising the lawn should continue even with organic care. The chemicals found in synthetic fertilisers are the same as those found in natural 'organic' type fertilisers. Do not let the word 'synthetic' confuse you. They are made from exactly the same elements as if natural but are simply more concentrated. This means that you will need to use far more quantities of a natural or 'organic' fertiliser as compared to a more concentrated synthetic fertiliser to get the same result. However, you should be aware that extremely heavy applications of nitrogen, phosphorus and potassium and other elements can lead to soil toxicities and eventual water pollution. Try to purchase products with low ratio's

i.e. 15:10:15 (15% Nitrogen – 10% Phosphorus – 15% Potassium) rather than those containing 30:15:30 or more as it is likely that the majority of the nutrient (especially Nitrogen) will be washed away before the plant roots have time to utilise them.

To make most efficient use of existing fertiliser levels in the soil you should not collect the clippings when mowing. Instead, return these to the lawn because it will eventually lead to re-cycling of the nutrient concentrations found in the cut leaf. Do not get confused with the old wives tale that returning clippings increases thatch levels. It will not - instead it will lead to a lusher, softer lawn. Fertilising should be carried out only when necessary. One way to keep fertiliser usage to a minimum is not to apply any until the grass leaves are exhibiting deficiency symptoms (see table 13).

IPM – INTEGRATED PEST MANAGEMENT

Integrated Pest Management is the use of alternative methods of control to reduce the amount of pesticides used.

IPM consists of combining specific management techniques such as:

- Cultural control measures
- Using resistant plant species
- Careful and considered use of fertiliser
- Use pesticides wisely
- Managing the soil correctly
- Using biological control methods
- Regularly inspecting the turf area
- Keeping your eye's open for new developments

Cultural

Good cultural management practices will mean that no chemical or biological methods are employed. Such as;

- Hand picking or hoeing weeds
- Planting grass species resistant (or that show some resistance) to the common diseases
- Scarifying thatch when necessary

- Aerating the soil adequately
- Maintaining adequate nutrient supplies to the plant
- Use pesticides wisely
- Removing the morning dew from the grass
- Irrigating correctly
- Cutting correctly and frequently
- Maintaining good turf husbandry

By carrying out the above you will ensure that a vigorous, dense and competitive turf grass plant prevails and grows and thereby prevent a lot of problems.

Use of resistant plant species

Sometimes resistance can be bred into plant species to help combat the susceptibility to disease. In turf grass species there are currently experiments being carried out into the use of *endophytes* (fungi that are grown and contained within the grass plant to limit pest damage). It is thought that grass species containing these may be more effective in the control of certain diseases.

Careful and considered use of fertiliser

By using fertiliser wisely you should be able to control the growth rates of the turf grass plant. Over fertilising will not only lead to a soft, lush and disease ridden plant, but it is also environmentally unsound (see fertilisers pages 49-53). Only apply fertiliser when necessary and only during the growing season.

Use pesticides wisely

Always use chemicals with care and caution. In section on turf, we discussed pesticides extensively, but what are pesticides? The word 'pesticides' encompasses three categories:

a) Fungicides (used to control disease)

b) Herbicides (used to control weeds)

c) Insecticides (used to control pests)

If any pesticide is used you must consider the following;

- Is it specific to the problem you are encountering?

- Does it have a low residual quality (the time it stays active once in contact with the soil)?
- Does it have low toxicity to man and animal?

Indiscriminate use of 'fungicides' or employment of numerous 'preventative' fungicide treatments can lead to disease control problems (remember that once you have seen the disease on the plant leaf, this is the last stage of the disease cycle, therefore you are treating it in its last stage of development! – infection of the grass plant would have occurred a long time beforehand).

Over use of fungicides can lead to a number of problems such as: (a) development of fungicide resistant diseases; (b) kill off the beneficial fungi and bacteria in the soil; (c) encourage other diseases to grow; and, (d) can encourage extensive thatch build up.

Managing the soil correctly

Managing the soil for turf involves making sure the soil does not compact too much (if it does, aerate),

and ensuring the pH of the soil is suited to the grass species you would like to grow and nurture.

NOTE – *Do not be fooled into thinking that you can adjust the pH of your soil. The soil pH you have is the soil pH you will keep. To adjust a soils pH would involve either removing all the top soil and replacing with new OR would involve fully incorporating soil pH adjusting materials (lime or organic matter) throughout the entire top soil area. Any soil pH adjustments you may make with acidifying fertilisers, pesticides, etc. will only ever affect the surface pH.*

Ensure that any top-dressings you apply to the grassed area are compatible with the soil below (i.e. adding a clay top dressing to a sandy soil is unadvisable)

Use of biological control measures
Keeping your eye's open for new developments

Biological control generally means the introduction of one organism

to control another. In turf there is limited use for this. However, there is research ongoing that may result in a change to the current situation regarding market availability.

Some known examples are:

PSEUDOMONAS BACTERIA for control of disease

AEROBIC BACTERIA for treatment of soil layering conditions

ENTOMOPATHOGENIC NEMATODES for treatment of turf pests

Presently, there are very few biological control methods available for private use. However, by keeping your eye's open for new developments in large garden centres and on the internet, you may find that a number of new techniques for pest control will become widely available in time.

TOP TURF TIP NO. 1
Watering Your Turf

Why Water?

All plants require lots and lots of water. The grasses on your turf are no different. The grass plant needs water as it forms over 80% of its entire make-up; only around 15% of the grass plant is actually dry matter.

Water is an essential component of photosynthesis and without it the grass cannot make food for growth and development. It is used to transport nutrients around the plant. The water inside the plant cells actually makes it stand upright (acts like our skeleton) and without this water the plant will wilt and eventually die. Over 90% of the water taken up by the plant is lost back to the atmosphere. Most water taken up is only used to cool the plant only before being released back into the atmosphere.

It is therefore essential to keep up the soils reserves in order to maintain a dense, uniform and aesthetically pleasing turf. If the plant is to produce a deep and extensive root system the soil must have water in it as this acts as a stimulus for root growth. With correct watering practices the grass plant will develop a deep and extensive root system that eventually leads to it being very drought resistant, allowing the plant to recover rapidly from wear and maintain good colour throughout the year.

How is the water lost?

Water in the soil is lost in two ways: Firstly, after water has entered the plant through the root system it travels upward to the plant leaves and is eventually lost to the atmosphere through thousands of tiny opening on the leaves called stomata. This action of water loss is termed transpiration. Secondly, water is lost from any exposed soil surface between the grass plants. This is termed evaporation. Together (Evapotranspiration) these processes account for the majority of the water lost from the soil.

A deficiency of water in the soil leads to a situation where water loss from the plant through transpiration exceeds what can be taken up by the roots; this causes stress to the grass plant. If this stress persists for more than a few days wilting may occur, the grass will dry out and brown patches may develop on the turf.

How should I apply water?

The obvious thing to say here is "water when the soil is in a dry state". Though, it is advised to water your turf heavily and infrequently. Generally the lighter the soil (the more sandy) the more water will need to be applied. The heavier the soil (Clayey) the less water will need to be applied.

Heavy application of water once every one - two weeks (depending upon weather) during the growing season with perhaps further lighter applications every 3 – 5 days in-between will encourage your grasses to maintain good top-growth, density and colour. Keep a check on the weather as you do not want to be over-watering the turf, not only does this waste water but it can also encourage the plant to produce shallow roots (the roots do not have to work to access water as it is always available on the surface!)

The benefits:

1. Your turf will be drought resistant
2. The grasses will retain better colour throughout the year
3. The turf will recover from wear at a much faster rate
4. The turf will become more resistant to attack from pests and diseases
5. A healthy, thick turf discourages the growth of many problem weeds

TOP TURF TIP NO. 2
Vertical Mowing (Scarification)

What is vertical mowing?

Scarification or vertical mowing is a cultural procedure (environmentally friendly) that involves the use of a machine that has a set of rapidly rotating knives or tines mounted on a shaft. The operation offers many benefits to your turf.

The machine used for this is around the size of a standard turf mower. Scarification can be carried out any time of the year as long as the grass is growing strongly enough to recover.

Why scarify?

The main purpose of scarification is to remove an organic material that occurs naturally just below the turf grass leaves, but above the soil layer. Scarification removes thatch and moss and helps promote a thick, lush grass surface.

What is thatch?

Thatch is an organic layer consisting of dead, dying and living stems, roots and leaves, in fact, all parts of the grass plant. A thick thatch layer will have a number of detrimental effects on any grass surface, including a soft, spongy surface and it proves to be an ideal breading ground for turf diseases and pests!

Thatch will also promote the ideal conditions for weed invasion, mosses and the growth of undesirable grass species. Thatch can also trap within it any nutrients applied to a turf resulting in a very shallow root system. Shallow rooted grasses offers poor drought resistance, colour and density and the plants ability to recover from wear will be drastically reduced.

The benefits?

Scarification should be carried out for a number of reasons

1. Reduces the amount of moss in the turf
2. Increases the density of the turf grasses
3. Removes undesirable thatch layers
4. Allows water and nutrients and oxygen access to the soil layers resulting in a healthier more drought resistant turf
5. Improves water infiltration rates of the soil
6. Creates the correct conditions needed for the germination of newly sown seed
7. Reduces water run-off from the turf surface
8. Prevents the formation of algae

TOP TURF TIP No. 3
Overseeding

What is over seeding?

Over seeding is the process of applying new seed to an already existing stand of grass. It can be carried out on small worn areas or across the whole turfed surface. Over sowing seed is an ideal way to produce a thick healthy turf that looks good the whole year through.

Over sowing is also carried out to replace the annual grass species found in many turfs that simply die off each year. All grasses naturally produce and lay seed when they flower each year (through production of a seed head), but, if a turf is mown then the grass is prevented from producing this due to the low height of cut forced upon it by the mower.

Why over seed?

Over seeding is carried out for the following reasons:

- A thick lush turf is required
- To allow the sowing of desirable grass seed such as species that are drought resistant, especially wear resistant, tolerate shade or simply retain a better winter colour
- Where the present standard of turf grass species is so poor that routine maintenance cannot improve it
- Because with constant mowing the grass is unable to produce seed-heads to reproduce itself!

When should I over seed?

Over sowing of new grass seed should be carried out from Spring until Autumn time. Any seed sown during the warmer summer months will need to be thoroughly watered throughout any prolonged hot, dry periods. The best time to over sow is the Autumn as at this time of year the soil is warm and the amount of natural rainfall is increased. Sowing in the Autumn will also allow the plant to develop an extensive root system through the winter period.

Over seeding is best carried out after Scarification, as this maintenance procedure allows the seed to integrate into the sward and aid the germination process.

The benefits?

1. Allows suitable grass species to adapt to your turf
2. Increases the density and improves the turfs texture
3. Ensures that the turf says healthy throughout the year and maintains good colour
4. With increased density the turf will actually suppress he growth of weeds
5. Sowing drought resistant grasses can decrease the amount of water that needs to be applied to the turf

TOP TURF TIP NO. 4
Aeration

What is aeration?

Aeration is the process of cultivating the soil beneath the grassed surface without disrupting the turfs surface characteristics. Most soils will need aeration if they receive wear from traffic be it human or mechanical.

Traffic on a turf compresses the soil beneath. This compression or compaction of the soil particles reduces the pore spaces between them. Compaction reduces the amounts of available oxygen that is held within the pore structure that is so vital for root growth, water movement and general plant health.

Any decrease in the size and number of soil pores will lead to many detrimental effects on the grass surface above. Drainage rates will be reduced and the rate at which water enters (infiltrates) the soil will also decrease, meaning a wet, soggy, un-usable turf for long periods after rain or through the winter period. Heavy compaction actually prevents the grass plant rooting as the pore spaces in the soil are too small to allow any roots to penetrate.

Compaction leads to many problems including:

- Increased amounts lateral surface rooting leading to increased amounts of thatch
- Poor summer colour is exhibited by the grass leaves
- Poor drought resistance of the plant
- Poor wear tolerance of the plant
- Ineffective use of water and fertilisers
- Can lead to an increase in moss

Why aerate?

If carried out correctly aeration will increase the levels of oxygen in the soil so vital to healthy root growth.

Aeration increases the soils ability to absorb water, preventing flooding and making the best use of any water applied.

Aeration will help breakdown the thatch layer while also ensuring that any fertiliser applied can gain access to the soil.

Aeration allows the incorporation of top-dressing to key into the soil surface but, perhaps the most beneficial effect of aeration is that when carried out correctly the operation is environmentally friendly, has no detrimental effect on your turf and the benefits the entire turf surface.

When is this done?

Aeration can essentially be carried out at any time of the year. Aeration should not be carried out when the soil is in a wet, saturated condition. Aeration of a wet soil leads to smearing when the tines are pushed in and pulled out. Smearing seals the soil preventing any air and/or water movement. Essentially this will cancel out all the benefits aeration brings.

TOP TURF TIP NO. 5
General Advice

. . . .

Mowing

Mowing is the most frequently carried out and the most fundamental practice utilised in turf maintenance. It is a defoliation process in which a portion of the turf grass leaf is 'removed'. Any cutting or defoliation is detrimental to the turf. The turf grass plant is able to survive mowing through continual leaf growth. The cut tip of a leaf proves to be an ideal site for entry and the penetration of pathogens into the grass plant.

Raising the height of cut of your turf mower by as little as 1 mm will aid the grass plant. Any increase in mowing height increases the rate and net amount of photosynthesis benefiting the overall health and development of the plant.

Seed mixtures

Different grass seed mixes (or blends as they are sometimes referred to) are used to create turfs for a number of reasons. Mixing grass genus and species offers benefits to the grower as it allows traits such as differences in texture to be introduced giving a dense characteristic to the sward.

We can specify individual grasses that may be resistant to shade, drought or wear to make the turf highly adaptable and help increase its survivability. Colour is another feature that can be specified, as is the tolerance to low mowing heights.

Moss

Mosses are beautiful plants in their own right; unfortunately though when present in turf they tend to look unsightly, make mowing difficult. Moss attracts water and can become hazardous underfoot. Mosses also tend to out-compete the desirable grass species during cooler seasons. There are some 600 species of moss in the United Kingdom and around 30 that are commonly found in turf.

The following factors favour the growth of moss:

- Moist soils
- Very dry soils
- Setting your mower too low aids moss growth and development due to the weak growth from the turf grass plant
- Soft, spongy, thatchy turfs
- High levels of compaction
- Constant or heavy shade on the turf
- Low fertility (lack of nutrients)

Moss on hard or paved areas can be killed with an application of a product containing ferrous sulphate or sulphate of iron.

Worms

Of the hundreds of different species of worms only three are responsible for producing the casts you see on your turf. These casts smother the grass when mowing, provide an ideal site for weed seeds to develop and grow whilst also looking unsightly. However, the benefits of worms far out-weigh the disadvantages. Worms consume thatch and provide aeration channels with their burrowing. These channels allow gaseous exchange to take place between the soil and atmosphere and help expel many harmful gases that build up in the soil. The channels also aid the drainage rate of your turf helping it to dry out after rain.

GLOSSARY

Acid soil – Soils whose pH is below 7 (Also see pH)

Aeration – Incorporating air into a soil; usually carried out by mechanical methods

Alkaline soil – Soils whose pH is above 7 (Also see pH)

Annual, summer – Plant that completes its life cycle from seed in one growing season

Annual, winter – Plant that initiates growth during the autumn, lives over winter, and dies after producing seed the following season

Blade – The flattened portion of the leaf located above the sheath

Brush – A device used that brushes the grass leaf and lifts the grass blades

Bunch-type growth – Plant developing itself through tillering at or near the soil surface without the production of stolons or rhizomes

Carbohydrate – The plants food source, a compound of carbon, hydrogen and oxygen, the end products being sugar, starch and cellulose

Castings (Earthworm) – Soil and plant remains excreted on the surface by earthworms.

Clippings – The parts of the grass plant deposited on the turf surface after mowing

Coring – A method of turf cultivation by which soil cores are removed using hollow tines and deposited on the surface

Compaction – The compression of soil particles leading to the starvation of oxygen in the soil structure

Crown – A compressed stem located at the base of a vegetative aerial shoot

Culm – Flower stem of the grass plant

Cultivar – An assemblage of cultivated plants distinguished by any characters (morphological, physiological, and the like) that when reproduced sexually or asexually retain their distinguishing features.

Cultivation – Applied to turf grass areas; cultivation refers to the manual/mechanical working of the soil and/or thatch layers without disturbing too greatly the turf grass surface

Evapotranspiration – Loss of water/moisture from the turf grass leaf and the soil surface

Grain – (Or 'nap') Grass laying uniformly in the same direction – general consequence of mowing

Irrigation, automatic – Control of water application in response to turf grass needs.

Irrigation, manual – Irrigation using hand hand-held equipment

Layering, soil – Undesirable layers within the surface horizons of a soil profile; can be due to frequently aerating the soil to the same depth, and/or frequently top-dressing with different textured materials.

Leaching – The loss of nutrients through natural drainage of the soil

Liquid fertilisation – A method of applying fertiliser using liquid as the carrier; always applied as a solution.

Mat – A tightly intermingled layer composing of dead, living and partially decomposed stem and root material and top soil, this layer develops below the grass blades but above the soils surface

Micro organism – Minute living organisms; such as bacteria or fungi

Mowing frequency – The number of times a turf is mown per week, month or growing season.

Mowing height – The distance above the ground at which the leaf is cut by a mowers blade.

Mulch – Any organic, or non-organic material that forms a covering on the turf grass or soil surface

Nitrification – Formation of nitrates and nitrites from ammonia by a soil's micro organisms

Perennial – A grass plant that lives for one or more growing seasons.

pH – literally means 'per hydrogen'; or 'the negative logarithm of the hydrogen ion concentration of the soil'

Root zone – A pre-mixed mixture of minerals and organic matter used as a growth medium for turf grass; can also be used to describe the top-soil

Rhizome – An elongated stem (or shoot) that grows underneath the surface of the ground and from which leaves and adventitious roots develop at the nodes

Settling, soil – A lowering of the soil surface resulting in a decrease of the total (aerated) volume of it. This can occur naturally but can also be accelerated by heeling in the surface after soil-cultivations have taken place.

Slowly available fertiliser – Designates a rate of dissolution less than normal for fertilisers; may involve organic and inorganic compounds that dissolve slowly.

Soil modification – Alteration of a soil's characteristics; commonly used to improve a soil's physical conditions to improve root growth of the grass plant

Soil probe – A soil sampling tool, that physically removes a portion of a soil – usually to allow testing to be carried out

Spiking – A method of turf cultivation in which solid tines or flat pointed blades; these penetrate the turf and soil surface – the simplest form of spiking is that of using a garden fork.

Stolon – An elongated stem (or shoot) that grows along the surface of the ground and from which leaves and adventitious roots develop at the nodes

Sub-soil – The soil found directly below the top soil. Sub-soil is not a good growing media for grasses due to its inert or toxic nature.

Switching – Sweeping of a grassed area to remove the morning dew of other materials

Texture, soil – The varying amounts of mineral matter found in soil – sand, silt clay or organic matter

Thatch – A layer of un-decomposed or partially decomposed organic residues situated above the soil surface but below the turf grass leaves.

Thatch control – The process of preventing excessive thatch build up or removing excess thatch from a turf surface using either mechanical or biological methods.

Tiller – A lateral shoot, usually erect that develops from buds

Top-dressing – A prepared soil mix added to the surface of a turf and worked in by brushing, raking and/or irrigating to produce a smooth surface. A well worked in top dressing can also accelerate thatch decomposition.

Tufted – A grass that develops new leaves from its base only

Turf – A covering of mown vegetation, usually turf grass.

Turf grass- A species or cultivar of grass, usually of spreading habit, that can be maintained as a mown turf

Turf grass community – A collection of individual turf grass plants (usually different species) that grow together

Urea formaldehyde – A synthetic, slowly soluble nitrogen fertiliser consisting mainly of methylene urea polymers

Vertical mower – A mechanical device that cuts into the turfgrass surface using vertically rotating blades - for the purpose of reducing thatch, and improving the exchange of gasses with the atmosphere.

Wear – The injurious effects of traffic (foot or mechanical) on the turf grass leaf blades.

Notes